Resurrecting Respect
True Patriotism

DAVE FITTON

Table of Contents

Table of Contents

Preface

Our country has fallen from a position of leadership and respect that it had earned after WW II. What made the U.S.A. the example for the rest of the world has eroded. The reasons are complex and not the work of any one political party or faction. The "blame game" runs rampant and as a result we have not been willing to work toward reclaiming our status. This little book attempts to examine the issues with an apolitical view. While the first part is essentially a "moan" the second part offers many practical solutions.

All of the following opinions and solutions support the following principals. If you have a problem with several of them, I suggest you stop reading and pass the book along to a friend (or enemy):

1. In the USA, our citizens and permanent residents deserve freedom of speech, worship and freedom from want & fear, affordable quality healthcare, and an affordable education.
2. Over time, many of our past successes have eroded and now require evaluation and change. There are many areas where we were once an (if not "the") world leader, but are no longer. Changes will be required to make the U.S.A. great again.
3. Our founding fathers intended to create a system where the common people ruled and not the "Royals." We have created a new class of Royals, if not in the title, but for certain in practice.
4. Service to country (and the earth) is more important than individual gain.
5. Individual freedoms are sacrosanct as long as they do not infringe on the right's other individuals
6. Short term benefits should never unduly mortgage future generations.

7. Government spending should be accountable to the taxpayer, and borrowing obligations should be "transparent" both in terms of current deficits and future "unfunded" liabilities. Both areas should be subject to reasonable limits that congress would not have the ability to override.

8. Unskilled and semi-skilled workers should receive, at a minimum, the compensation required to provide the entitlements in #1 above.

9. When the economy (real GDP) is growing the middle class deserves its fair share of this growth. The middle class is paying more than their fair share to fund our government.

10. Persons and families in need deserve our support. We should give those in need the opportunity to maintain their self-respect. Everyone should have the opportunity to "contribute" to the country commensurate to their abilities. All subsidies should have limited terms except in cases of ongoing and legally documented disability.

11. The role of money in our election process and determining the outcome must be reduced.

12. Least government is the best government. Citizens in service to the Federal Government will be paid fairly, but not overpaid. By that, I mean their total compensation should be in line with comparable positions in private industry. Where possible, productivity standards should be in place for all government workers.

13. The time available for election campaigns requires reduction. We need more time governing and less time campaigning.

14. Capitalism is the preferred economic system as long as it provides for most of the citizens to participate in owning capital. Participation in capitalism should include all classes other than those requiring subsidies.

15. Taxes come in many forms. For example: When your government chooses to support an inefficient and costly system when cheaper and better alternatives exist, then you are being taxed.

16. Worldwide free markets are most efficient in the long-term, fostering innovation and productivity

17. Growth for the sake of growth is not the best measure of economic viability. Productivity ultimately determines effective resource utilization

and well-being. This measure becomes even more important for countries when their internal population is declining. Measures like GDP per capita are a better economic measure of success.

18. Our elected representatives should play by the same rules as the voters that elected them into office regarding benefits and entitlements.

This book contains two Parts. Part one explores several of the areas that are preventing us from being a world leader. Part two presents reasonable and affordable remedies (and ones that have bipartisan support among the voters for the most part)

PART ONE

PART ONE

CHAPTER 1:

The Beginning, the Constitution & Amendments

Our Founding Fathers' did an admirable job constructing our Constitution and the initial ten amendments (AKA the bill of rights). They were smart enough to realize that circumstances would change over time and allowed for a process to amend the initial document. Excerpt from the Constitution:

"Article. V. - Amendment

The Congress, whenever two thirds of both Houses shall deem it necessary, shall propose Amendments to this Constitution, or, on the Application of the Legislatures of two thirds of the several States, shall call a Convention for proposing Amendments, which, in either Case, shall be valid to all Intents and Purposes, as part of this Constitution, when ratified by the Legislatures of three fourths of the several States, or by Conventions in three fourths thereof, as the one or the other Mode of Ratification may be proposed by the Congress; Provided that no Amendment which may be made prior to the Year One thousand eight hundred and eight shall in any Manner affect the first and fourth Clauses in the Ninth Section of the first Article; and that no State, without its Consent, shall be deprived of its equal Suffrage in the Senate."

Unfortunately, our founders did not anticipate the advent of the career politician and their future ability to repress the amendment process in the face of overwhelming public support for change. It is especially evident when it comes to items that would specifically impact political longevity like term limits and modification to their pay and benefits. Recent polls indicate that over 80% of registered voters would support an amendment to limit congressional terms. Also, when establishing the house of representatives' terms, they would not envision that half of the 2-year term involves re-election campaigning.

At the time of drafting this book, 15 states have taken on the term limit issue for their elected officials. There is almost equal representation among "red" and "blue" states. On average, these issues received 67% of the vote. Most of the term limits are at eight years, with an overall average of 9.6. See the following chart:

State	Year Enacted	Limit	Year of Impact	Limit	Year of Impact	% Voted Yes
MAINE	1993	8	1996	8	1996	67.6
CALIFORNIA	1990	12	1996	12	1998	52.2
COLORADO	1990	8	1998	8	1998	71
ARKANSAS	1992	16	1998	16	2000	59.9
MICHIGAN	1992	6	1998	8	2002	58.8
FLORIDA	1992	8	2000	8	2000	76.8
OHIO	1992	8	2000	8	2000	68.4
SOUTH DAKOTA	1992	8	2000	8	2000	63.5
MONTANA	1992	8	2000	8	2000	67
ARIZONA	1992	8	2000	8	2000	74.2
MISSOURI (a)	1992	8	2002	8	2002	75
OKLAHOMA	1990	12	2004	12	2004	67.3
NEBRASKA	2000	n/a	n/a	8	2006	56
LOUISIANA	1995	12	2007	12	2007	76
NEVADA (b)	1996	12	2010	12	2010	70.4
		9.6				**67%**

After FDR was elected four times, terms were limited. He was arguably one of, if not the, most popular president. His approval rating when he left office was 70 percent and the percentage point difference between the beginning and end of his terms was +9. His average approval rating was 64 percent

FDR left the office with the highest approval rating out of any of the thirteen Presidents on record. He's also one of the only two presidents to leave the office with more popularity than when he left. The only other was Bill Clinton. Our legislators had the vision to understand that it is never the intent of our constitution to have a long-term leader, and they facilitated the adoption of the 22nd Amendment in 1947.

There were no term limits when George Washington was elected. There were also no approval rating systems in place at that time. I guess that his approval rating would have been the highest of all time since he was the only candidate that was elected by a unanimous vote. It is important to know that he did not seek a 3rd term, one that he would have been able to easily secure.

Thomas Jefferson; his view on congressional terms in a letter to S. Adams:

"A government by representatives elected by the people at short periods was our object, and our maxim... was, 'where annual election ends, tyranny begins;' nor have our departures from it been sanctioned by the happiness of their effects." –Thomas Jefferson to S. Adams, 1800."

President Washington did not subscribe to the idea of political parties and did not register with one. The warning he voiced in his farewell address regarding the two-party system was prophetic, and his mastery of our language is exceptional:

"The alternate domination of one faction over another, sharpened by the spirit of revenge, natural to party dissension, which in different ages and countries has perpetrated the most horrid enormities, is itself a frightful despotism. But this leads at length to a more formal and permanent despotism. The disorders and miseries, which result, gradually incline the minds of men to seek security and repose in the absolute

power of an individual; and sooner or later the chief of some prevailing faction, more able or more fortunate than his competitors, turns this disposition to the purposes of his own elevation, on the ruins of Public Liberty

Without looking forward to an extremity of this kind, (which nevertheless ought not to be entirely out of sight,) the common and continual mischiefs of the spirit of party are sufficient to make it the interest and duty of a wise people to discourage and restrain it.

It serves always to distract the Public Councils and enfeeble the Public Administration. It agitates the Community with ill-founded jealousies and false alarms; kindles the animosity of one part against another foments occasionally riot and insurrection. It opens the door to foreign influence and corruption, which find a facilitated access to the government itself through the channels of party passions. Thus, the policy and the will of one country are subjected to the policy and will of another.

There is an opinion, that parties in free countries are useful checks upon the administration of the Government, and serve to keep alive the spirit of Liberty. This within certain limits is probably true; and in Governments of a Monarchical cast, Patriotism may look with indulgence, if not with favor, upon the spirit of party. But in those of the popular character, in Governments purely elective, it is a spirit not to be encouraged. From their natural tendency, it is certain there will always be enough of that spirit for every salutary purpose. And, there being constant danger of excess, the effort ought to be, by force of public opinion, to mitigate and assuage it. A fire not to be quenched, it demands a uniform vigilance to prevent its bursting into a flame, lest, instead of warming, it should consume."

Washington was not the only one of our founding fathers that put forth this warning.

John Adams:

"There is nothing which I dread so much as a division of the republic into two great parties, each arranged under its leader, and concerting measures in opposition to each other. This, in my humble apprehension, is to be dreaded as the greatest political evil under our Constitution."

And Jefferson:

"Experience hath shewn, that even under the best forms (of government) those entrusted with power have, in time, and by slow operations, perverted it into tyranny"

In this chapter, I have raised two important issues that require change. There is one other significant issue. The national election process, and the role of time and money in determining the outcome and governing effectiveness.

CHAPTER 2:

Four Freedoms

The following are a few excerpts from FDR's address to the 77th members of Congress. The entire address is well worth the read, and I encourage you to view it. You can easily access it via a google search:

"A free nation has the right to expect full cooperation from all groups. A free nation has the right to look to the leaders of business, of labor, and of agriculture to take the lead in stimulating effort, not among other groups but within their own groups.

The best way of dealing with the few slackers or trouble makers in our midst is, first, to shame them by patriotic example, and, if that fails, to use the sovereignty of Government to save Government.

Certainly, this is no time for any of us to stop thinking about the social and economic problems which are the root cause of the social revolution which is today a supreme factor in the world.

For there is nothing mysterious about the foundations of a healthy and strong democracy. The basic things expected by our people of their political and economic systems are simple. They are:

Equality of opportunity for youth and for others.

- Jobs for those who can work.
- Security for those who need it.
- The ending of special privilege for the few.
- The preservation of civil liberties for all.
- The enjoyment of the fruits of scientific progress in a wider and constantly rising standard of living.

These are the simple, basic things that must never be lost sight of in the turmoil and unbelievable complexity of our modern world. The inner and abiding strength of our economic and political systems is dependent upon the degree to which they fulfill these expectations.

Many subjects connected with our social economy call for immediate improvement.

As examples:

We should bring more citizens under the coverage of old-age pensions and unemployment insurance.

We should widen the opportunities for adequate medical care.

We should plan a better system by which persons deserving or needing gainful employment may obtain it.

I have called for personal sacrifice. I am assured of the willingness of almost all Americans to respond to that call..

.................The Four Freedoms:

In the future days, which we seek to make secure, we look forward to a world founded upon four essential human freedoms.

- The first is freedom of speech and expression – everywhere in the world.
- The second is freedom of every person to worship God in his own

way – everywhere in the world.

- The third is freedom from want – which, translated into world terms, means economic understandings which will secure to every nation a healthy peacetime life for its inhabitants - everywhere in the world.
- The fourth is freedom from fear – which, translated into world terms, means a world-wide reduction of armaments to such a point and in such a thorough fashion that no nation will be in a position to commit an act of physical aggression against any neighbor - anywhere in the world.

That is no vision of a distant millennium. It is a definite basis for a kind of world attainable in our own time and generation.

To that new order, we oppose the greater conception – the moral order. A good society is able to face schemes of world domination and foreign revolutions alike without fear.

Since the beginning of our American history, we have been engaged in change – in a perpetual peaceful revolution - a revolution which goes on steadily, quietly adjusting itself to changing conditions – without the concentration camp or the quick-lime in the ditch. The world order which we seek is the cooperation of free countries, working together in a friendly, civilized society."

Source: The Public Papers and Addresses of Franklin D. Roosevelt, 1940: War and Aid to Democracies.

CHAPTER 3:

Lost Leadership

Once Great Britain was the world's power and led the world in many categories. Their method of land acquisition was not one that I admire, but it was effective. Times changed, and they gradually lost their position in the world. During and after WW II, our country quite quickly took the lead in many areas and along with the Soviet Union assumed Super Power status. At the time, we had about the same populations (3rd & 4th after China & India). Two different systems competed for status. Capitalism spawned a large and prosperous "middle-class." Communism was effective in certain areas (like controlling the masses), but was not conducive to accelerating productivity and thus the best living standards. The Soviet system eventually crumbled, and Russia lost both influence and population.

At the peak of US influence, we were world leaders in the standard of living, per capita GDP (productivity), quality of life, longevity & near the top concerning the quality of healthcare. We no longer rank at the top in any of these areas.

The following chart is from 2018 and shows how we have slipped from our top spot, and I suspect that we have declined from the # 8 position since that time.

Source: International Monetary Fund World Economic Outlook March 2018

Country	Per Capita GDP 2018
1 Luxembourg	$ 115,203
2 Macao SAR	$ 86,339
3 Switzerland	$ 85,157
4 Norway	$ 82,773
5 Iceland	$ 79,271
6 Ireland	$ 77,160
7 Qatar	$ 72,677
8 United States	$ 65,062
9 Singapore	$ 62,984
10 Denmark	$ 62,041
11 Australia	$ 57,204
12 Sweden	$ 54,135
13 Netherlands	$ 54,129
14 Austria	$ 52,474
15 San Marino	$ 51,029
16 Finland	$ 50,879
17 Hong Kong SAR	$ 50,567
18 Germany	$ 49,692
19 Canada	$ 48,601
20 Belgium	$ 47,532

We have slipped to 15th in the monetary standard of living, to 31st in longevity, 13th in overall quality of life (taking into account both monetary & numerous other factors) and alarmingly to 37th in quality of healthcare.

Our economic model has been on the decline since the late '80s at a time when the Soviet Union was in shambles and at a time when we had a distinct advantage. I'm sure that the political parties would like to place blame on their opponents. The truth is that both parties have had control for significant periods, and neither has managed to turn the tide of regression. They are too busy pointing fingers.

Have we become apathetic? I contend that we lack the leadership that made us such a formidable and admired country after WWII. The desire to maintain a congressional career has been significant contributing factor in the decline.

CHAPTER 4:

The Healthcare Tax

The average employee income in our country as of 2019 was $48,000, and the median family income was $63,000. In the county where I reside, the median family income was $38,000.

I site these numbers so you can evaluate them relative to the cost to subsist. Overall our highest cost is healthcare. It is much higher than the next highest which would be housing (mortgage [or rent], utilities, taxes, insurance, maintenance, etc. included)

As of 2019, the per capita cost of healthcare in the US exceeded $11,000 for every adult, child & infant. Our per capita cost for healthcare is almost three times the average of the EU Countries and more than what is required for a family to provide for all other essentials. Nationwide we are spending almost $3.5 trillion a year on healthcare.

If a family of four had to pay their average share of this cost, they would be facing almost $44,000 in expense. Reasonable funds are required to provide for basic housing, food, transportation, clothing, repairs & maintenance, insurance & a modest contingency fund. Anything less than a family income of $75,000 per annum will require some form of subsidy to cover the basics.

Currently, about 1/3 of the cost of healthcare is being funded by the government in the form of Medicare & Medicaid. Another 1/3 (or slightly more) is funded through company healthcare plans. Citizens are paying the remainder in the form of premiums, deductibles, and co-pays. From a company's point of view, this high cost to them reduces the funds available for wage compensation.

What is the point of this information? For our citizens to experience the four freedoms and any of the other entitlements, it tends to boil down to money. Additionally, it appears that the most significant barrier to achieving the ability to "afford" the freedoms/entitlements is the cost of healthcare. We should figure out how to achieve the average cost and quality of care experienced by EU or OECD countries. Were we to redistribute the excess funds it would cover all of the costs as well as all subsidies required. Why do our elected representatives focus on relatively meaningless plans that only tweak the existing system when the real issue should be <u>cost & quality of care?</u>

The folowing chart from 2018 displays just how out of control our healthcare costs have become

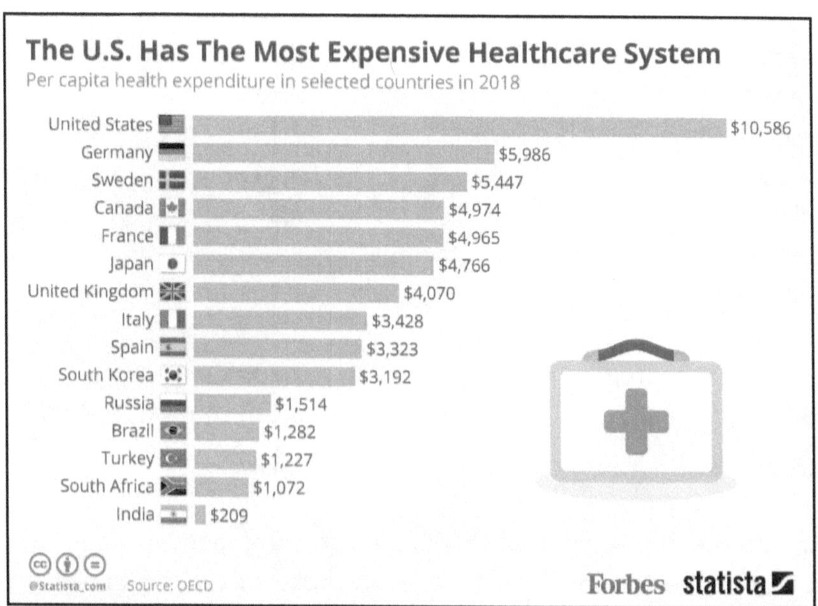

Politicians put forth the argument that while our healthcare cost is very high, it is worth it as we have the best healthcare in the world. <u>Not so</u>, according to the source: The World Health Organization! See the chart following:

Best Quality of Care Ranking	**2012 Per Capita Cost**
1 France	$3,974
2 Italy	2,962
7 Spain	3,076
9 Austria	4,395
10 Japan	3,035
11 Norway	5,388
12 Portugal	2,728
14 Greece	2,914
15 Iceland	3,309
17 Netherlands	5,056
18 United Kingdom	3,433
19 Ireland	3,718
20 Switzerland	5,270
21 Belgium	3,959
23 Sweden	3,756
25 Germany	4,338
28 Israel	2,165
30 Canada	4,445
31 Finland	3,251
32 Australia	3,670
33 Chile	1,202
34 Denmark	4,464
36 Costa Rica (approx.)	2,500
37 USA	8,233 (now @ $11,000)
AVERAGE	**3,266**

You can do the math as easily as I. We are currently spending about $3.5 trillion a year on healthcare. Over time, if we chose to cut this in half, it would easily fund the 20% of our citizens who do not have healthcare coverage today. There would be enough left over to balance the Federal Budget and still have some leftover to fund several very worthwhile efforts for the common good.

This chapter will be the longest in this book and for a good reason. Why are our healthcare costs so out of control? Here are some of the facts:

RX Drugs: American consumers pay roughly 3000 percent more than the actual manufacturing costs for prescription drugs. We are the only nation that does not have price controls and negotiate our drug prices. In a sense, we are bearing the cost of the world's R&D. The prices Americans pay are excessive and, in fact, drug companies are increasingly pocketing their huge profits rather than reinvesting them. For example, in 2002, 78 new drugs were approved by the FDA. Of those, only 17 were deemed by the FDA to have new active ingredients, and only seven were found to be improvements over the older drugs. On top of that, of the seven found to be an improvement over the older drug, not one of them came from U.S. companies.

Legal Factors: Ambulance chasing has reached new heights. If you watch any TV, you will witness the most recent form of abuse. It is difficult to watch even a couple of hours of TV without seeing a law firm seeking participants in a class-action suit against a drug company for compensation. It is not my place to judge the efficacy of any of these drugs. I suspect that many are very harmful. I am addressing the cost to our health care system. These suits translate into higher insurance costs, all of which are passed along to the consumer. The USA leads the world in malpractice & bad drug lawsuits. We have the highest per capita ratio of lawyers in the world. I'm not sure this is a good thing. My take on this is that we produce too many lawyers. They need to create demand for their services to take advantage of their education (and also possibly to pay back student loans). Again, I'm do not mean to excuse the responsibility to produce safe meds.

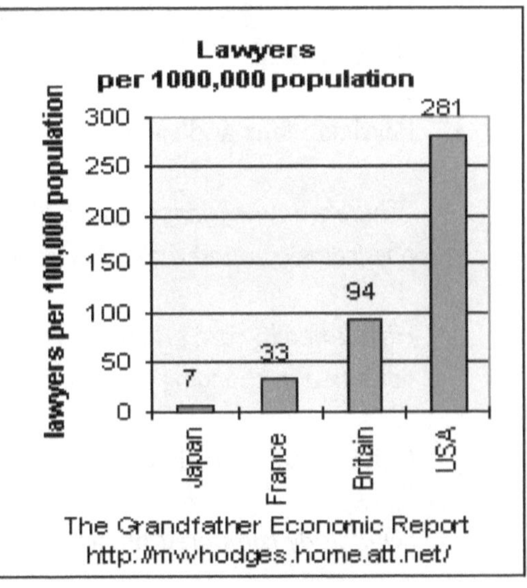

The Grandfather Economic Report
http://mwhodges.home.att.net/

Another example is the high number of physician malpractice suits in the US. This increases insurance premiums, which eventually get passed along to the consumer.

The main driver of medical malpractice costs is the practice area. Doctors in internal medicine pay an average of $4,000 to $6,000 annually for medical malpractice insurance, according to the Insurance QnA website. Surgeons pay an average of $10,000 to $15,000 in annual premiums. Specialty physicians like OB/GYNS can expect to pay annual premiums between $15,000 and $20,000

Cost of Physicians: In our community, as in most, doctors are among the wealthiest. As Americans, we place a very high value on the person that looks after our physical well-being. It's too bad that we do not place the same value on maintaining that well-being. No price is too high. Combine that attitude with the assumption that we are receiving a high level of quality care and you begin to see the problem. Add one more factor that many physicians attempt to maximize their earnings to support the lifestyle that they enjoy. What this leads to is that we have the highest physician cost among all reporting countries:

> Source of below: http://theincidentaleconomist.com/wordpress/physician-fees-and-salaries-in-the-us-and-other-countries/ by Aaron Carroll

- Physician fees and salaries in the US and other countries

> *"There's a new manuscript in Health Affairs on the higher fees paid to US physicians compared to other countries. Let's work through the abstract:*

> *Higher health care prices in the United States are a key reason that the nation's health spending is so much higher than that of other countries."*

> Can't argue with that!

> *"Our study compared physicians' fees paid by public and private payers for*

primary care office visits and hip replacements in Australia, Canada, France, Germany, the United Kingdom, and the United States. We also compared physicians' incomes net of practice expenses, differences in financing the cost of medical education, and the relative contribution of payments per physician and of physician supply in the countries' national spending on physician services.

Fees are the amount paid to the doctor's office for a visit, or to surgeons for their services. This is different from salaries, of course, as overhead and infrastructure should be bundled in fees.

Public and private payers paid somewhat higher fees to US primary care physicians for office visits (27 percent more for public, 70 percent more for private) and much higher fees to orthopedic physicians for hip replacements (70 percent more for public, 120 percent more for private) than public and private payers paid these physicians' counterparts in other countries. US primary care and orthopedic physicians also earned higher incomes ($186,582 and $442,450, respectively) than their foreign counterparts. We conclude that the higher fees, rather than factors such as higher practice costs, the volume of services, or tuition expenses, were the main drivers of higher US spending, particularly in orthopedics.

So, not surprisingly, things cost more in the US. Way more. This is when I say that this would be OK (potentially) if the outcomes or quality were so much better in the US. They're not. It would also be explained if the US was doing more per visit, doing more services, or if costs were higher. They're not. It's just the fees.

I think most news, however, will focus on the salaries of physicians in the US. They're higher than in other countries."

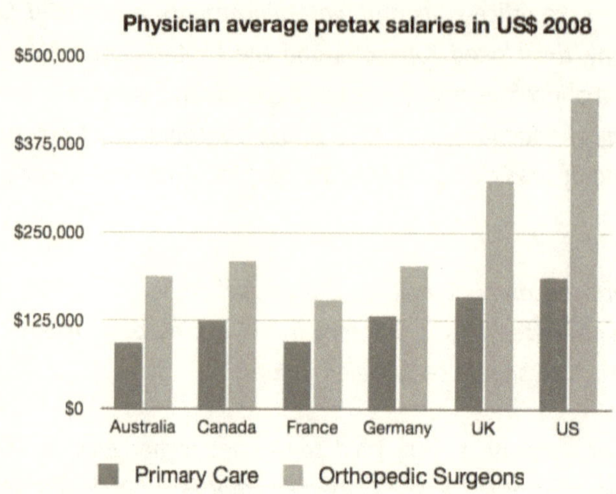

How about a basic doctor's appointment? In the U.S., the average price is $95, and it ranges to $176 or more. In second-place is Chile, at $38.

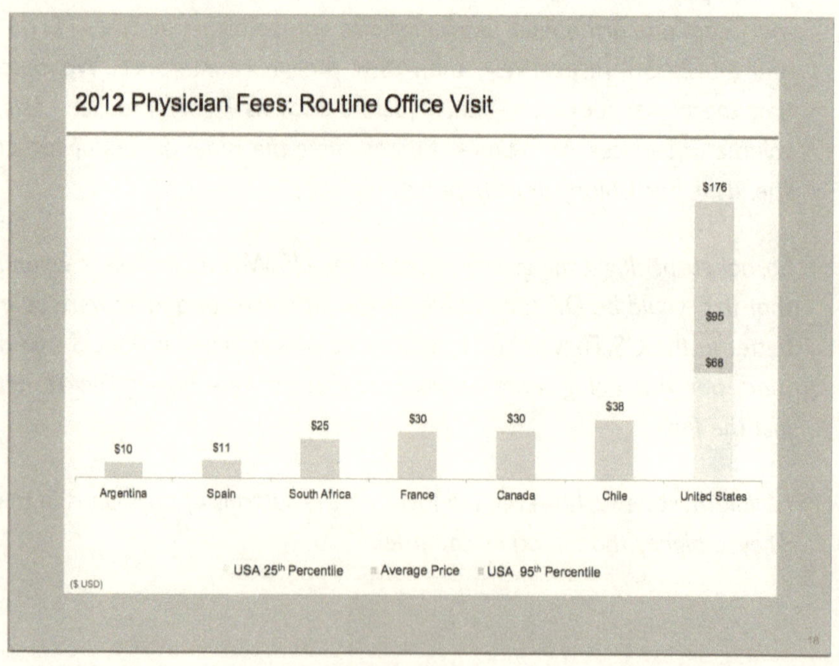

Hospitals: There are numerous documented examples of hospital financial abuse in this country. Overcharges for OTC medications, overprescribed testing, and phantom charges are among these examples. In the US we pay more for hospital services than in any other country. Do we receive superior care in exchange? Considering where we rank in terms of quality of care, it is doubtful:

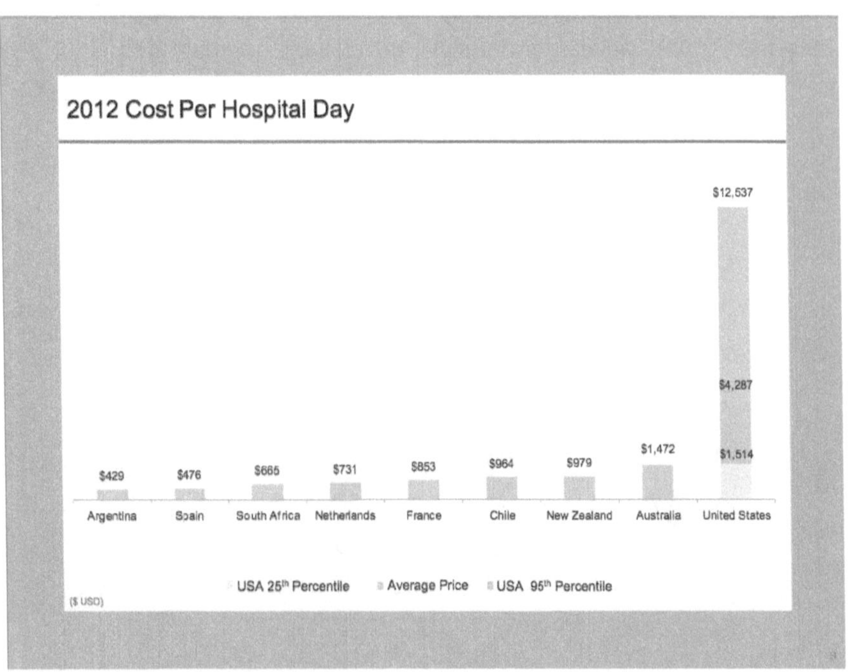

Source: http://imgur.com/6AixGOS

The preceding chart says it all!

Insurance Companies:

In almost all situations, my view is that the private sector outperforms public attempts. I am convinced that healthcare is an exception.

Insurance companies' primary concerns, like any large corporation, are quarterly earnings reports and the price of their stock. They are more motivated to increase premiums and reduce their costs. Improving the quality of care or reducing the actual cost to consumers is not part of their incentives. It appears that in other countries' single-payer systems (many also allow for private option) foci on quality of care and making it affordable. It also appears that a much higher % of the money spent goes towards proving actual care and not into profits and high administrative costs. See the chart below.

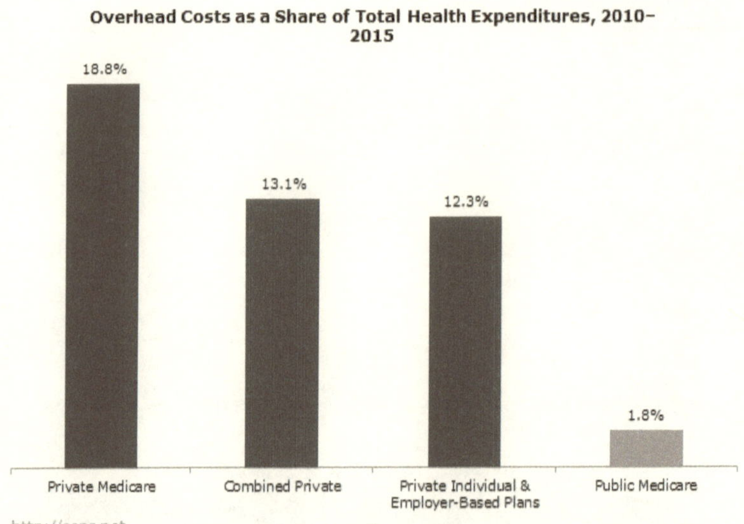

http://cepr.net
Source: Centers for Medicare & Medicaid Services; Medicare Trustees Reports, 2011–2016.

Spending on Health Education, is it working?

Your government spends an enormous amount of money on Health Education each year. The accepted opinion is that the best way to improve individual health (and reduce costs) is to ensure that the public is informed. The importance of a proper diet and exercise to longevity and quality of life is stressed. However, the facts do not support this assumption. Despite spending increasing Billions of dollars each year (yes with a __B__), the population is not becoming healthier. One good indicator is the rate of obesity:

Obesity in the United States

From Wikipedia, the free encyclopedia

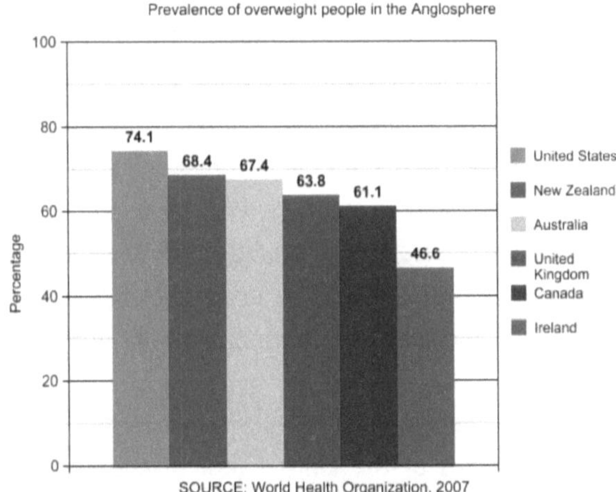

According to 2007 statistics from the World Health Organization (WHO), the United States has the highest prevalence of overweight adults in the Anglosphere.

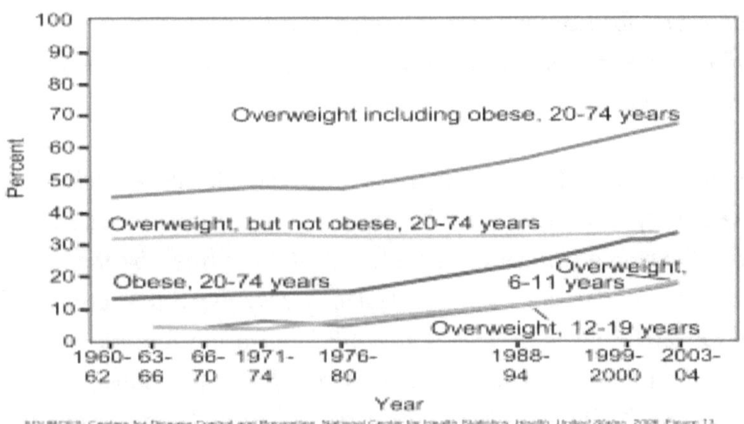

Historical U.S. obesity rate, 1960–2004[1]
Source: http://en.wikipedia.org/wiki/Obesity_in_the_United_States

"Obesity in the United States has been increasingly cited as a major health issue in recent decades. While many industrialized countries have experienced similar increases, obesity rates in the United States are among the highest in the world.

Obesity has continued to grow within the United States. Two out of every three Americans are considered to be overweight or obese. During the early 21st century, America often contained the highest percentage of obese people in the world. Obesity has led to over 120,000 preventable deaths each year in the United States. An obese person in America is likely to incur $1,497 more in medical expenses annually. Approximately $190 billion is spent in added medical expenses per year within the United States. Obesity is a preventable condition that has been increasing within the United States. Health authorities anticipate no change to this vector.

The United States had the highest rate of obesity for large countries until obesity rates in Mexico surpassed that of the United States in 2013. From 13% obesity in 1962, estimates have steadily increased. The following statistics comprise adults age 20 and over living at or near the poverty level. The obesity percentages for the overall US population are higher. reaching 19.4% in 1997, 24.5% in 2004, 26.6% in 2007, and 33.8% (adults) and 17% (children) in 2008. In 2010, the Centers for Disease Control and Prevention (CDC) reported higher numbers once more, counting 35.7% of American adults as obese, and 17% of American children. In 2013 the Organization for Economic Co-operation and Development (OECD) found that 27.6% of American citizens were obese. The organization estimates that 3/4 of the American population will likely be overweight or obese by 2020.

According to a study in The Journal of the American Medical Association (JAMA), in 2008, the obesity rate among adult Americans was estimated at 32.2% for men and 35.5% for women; these rates were roughly confirmed by the CDC again for 2009–2010. Using different criteria, a Gallup survey found the rate was 26.1% for U.S. adults in 2011, up from 25.5% in 2008. Though the rate for women has held steady over the previous decade, the obesity rate for men continued to increase between 1999 and 2008, the JAMA study notes. Moreover, "The prevalence of obesity for adults aged 20 to 74 years increased by 7.9 percentage points for men and by 8.9 percentage points for women between 1976–1980 and 1988–1994, and subsequently by 7.1 percentage points for men and by 8.1 percentage points for women between 1988–1994 and 1999–2000.

Obesity has been cited as a contributing factor to approximately 100,000–400,000 deaths in the United States per year and has increased health care use and expenditures, costing society an estimated $117 billion in direct (preventive, diagnostic, and treatment services related to weight) and indirect (absenteeism, loss of future earnings due to premature death) costs. This exceeds health-care costs associated with smoking or problem drinking and accounts for 6% to 12% of national health care expenditures in the United States."

Figure 5. Trends in obesity prevalence among adults aged 20 and over (age adjusted) and youth aged 2–19 years: United States, 1999–2000 through 2015–2016

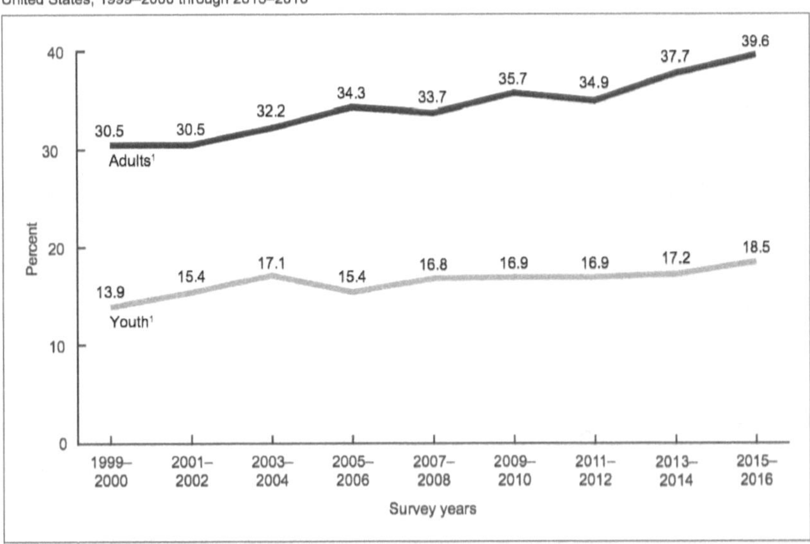

¹Significant increasing linear trend from 1999–2000 through 2015–2016.
NOTES: All estimates for adults are age adjusted by the direct method to the 2000 U.S. census population using the age groups 20–39, 40–59, and 60 and over.
Access data table for Figure 5 at: https://www.cdc.gov/nchs/data/databriefs/db288_table.pdf#5.
SOURCE: NCHS, National Health and Nutrition Examination Survey, 1999–2016.

To summarize, many factors contribute to our country's outrageous cost of providing healthcare. Since other countries can provide superior care at less than half the cost, the result is a massive regressive tax that is being borne by the middle class. Lower-income families are subsidized (in most instances) by taxpayers, and the cost factor is insignificant for the high-income group,

CHAPTER 5:

Changes in our Economy

Our country is based on the idea that it should not be up to the fortunate few to make the rules. The early economy was based primarily on farming. Many of the founding fathers were farmers and considered politics a part-time service to their country. I doubt they considered the possibility of a career politician.

Our revolution resulted from flawed economics and a lack of effective representation. We had been a colony of England, and they (by "they" I mean the Royals) made the rules. The slogan "taxation without representation" was used to incite emotion. The charge to revolt was led primarily by the merchant class. When visiting historical sites on the East Coast, their story was that at the time of the revolution about 1/3 of the population was in favor of leaving the British fold. Another 1/3 were loyalists (to the Crown), and another 1/3 were apathetic. I'm not sure how they took that poll. If folks were anything like they are today, I suspect that no more than 20% sided with either the Revolutionaries or the Loyalists and the remainder didn't have a clue.

The Revolution was a success, and the founders attempted to design a democratic Republic where the majority determine the rules through a system of three co-equal branches of government. The intention was that no branch should have more power than either of the other two through a system of checks and balances. Democracy would replace Autocracy.

Times change and the Industrial Revolution shifted the economy from agrarian domination to commercial dominance. Over time the concept of capitalism took hold. In the agrarian model, the primary source of capital was land, and the landowners were in control. The land was wealth and the source of income. When the economy shifted to commerce, other elements of capital came to fore. Land ownership was still a factor, but other citizens could participate as equipment and business ideas entered the equation. In the late 19th century, the stock market emerged, allowing many others to participate in equity ownership (capital) and share in the risk & rewards. The idea was this could be an effective way to broaden citizen participation in capitalism. It was a great idea, and at one-point, last century, over 65% of adults participated in a stock market. Today that rate has dropped to near 50%. There are a couple of factors at play. First, it takes the availability of discretionary income to be able to invest in capital opportunities. Middle-class disposable income has been relatively stagnant for the past few decades while expenses like healthcare and advanced education have been rising at alarming rates. Secondly, Mutual Funds and other large investment firms have become the more dominant owners of equities.

CHAPTER 6:

The New Royal Class

As a result of the preceding, we have spawned a new class of Royals comprised of the top 1 % of the wealthy, large company executives, investment firms, banks, and your elected representatives. The top 1% wealthiest control just under 40% and the top 10% control 75% of the capital and the income that it produces. The middle class controls a very small per cent of the country's capital. Our new Royal class is, in reality, an Oligarchy comprised of a small group that owns most of the capital and is in position to make the rules.

At the time of this narrative, our annualized GDP stood at $21.3 trillion, and our population stood at 328 million. Again, you can do the math. It amounts to $65,000 for every man woman & child. At the current average family size of 3.19 that amounts to almost exactly $200,000 per family. Much of the GDP needs to fund the cost of resources and capital investment (about half). But does it seem fair to the reader that a young family with both adults working at minimum wage receive less than $40,000 (20%) of what we produce?

We have a great economic system, but the question is how fairly do we "distribute" funds between capital and labor. The top 20% income group is currently receiving 46% of the funds allocated for labor compensation while the average in the EU is in the 36 – 37% range. It appears that there is some room for a more equitable distribution. This condition is exacerbated when some top CEOs are making upwards of 500 times as much as the average of their employees.

CHAPTER 7:

Service to Country

JFK may have been a rascal and morally compromised, but he did possess considerable leadership and oratory skills. His approval rating reached 77% one year after his inauguration. Probably one of his most quoted proclamations was:

"And so, my fellow Americans: ask not what your country can do for you, ask what you can do for your country. My fellow citizens of the world: ask not what America will do for you, but what, together, we can do for the freedom of man."

As patriots, we may not think we can have an impact on our country, but I disagree. All of us have the opportunity to contribute at the local level. Every community has numerous worthwhile community projects and non-profit efforts. They are always in need of volunteers. Grassroots efforts are important and benefit your community and ultimately, the country.

The most important action we can take is to put "labels" aside when it comes to problem-solving. If you are a political conservative, consider that not all "liberals" are idiots and that they have skills to offer our society. If you are a political progressive, consider that not all conservatives are extreme fascists and they also have valuable skills. My view is that more folks on the "right" and the "left" have opinions that are closer to the center than the extremes.

I am convinced that, given a chance, a group of ordinary citizens comprised of moderates from both sides (right & left) could compromise on a wide variety of the most important issues.

CHAPTER 8:

Individual Freedom

The Bill of Rights does a fine job of specifying the rights and freedoms that we should expect as citizens. The First Amendment covers quite a lot of ground concerning individual Freedoms:

"Congress shall make no law respecting an establishment of religion, or prohibiting the free exercise thereof, or abridging the freedom of speech, or of the press, or the right of the people peaceably to assemble, and to petition the Government for a redress of grievances."

The 9th Amendment tends to amend (or clarify) the 1st:

"The enumeration in the Constitution, of certain rights, shall not be construed to deny or disparage others retained by the people."

The above declarations form the backbone of the amended Constitution as determined by the founders. Many of the other amendments deal with legal issues. These freedoms became a model for many other countries that migrated from the domination of the Royals to a more democratic system.

I have a couple of concerns relative to this topic.

The first has to do with the press. Political personalities have never been happy when the press published articles that are critical of their actions. Most Presidents have experienced unflattering articles, and many have expressed their displeasure. When any political figure suggests that the press should not be allowed to express their opinions that would seem to violate the constitution (in my opinion). They would only be expressing their opinion, but that opinion seems to contradict the intention of the 1ˢᵗ amendment.

The second has to do with certain groups that express their opinion that our country should only be occupied by their preferred group. Again, they are only expressing an opinion, but that opinion seems to violate both the content and intention of the Constitution. When those opinions resort to hate and advocate violence, then in my view this meets the definition of terrorism.

CHAPTER 9:

The Short-term vs. Long-term & Unfunded Liabilities

One significant issue that has kept us from maintaining our elite status is that we have had a very short-term focus. Most public companies tend to make decisions that maximize their performance from one quarter to the next. Many political decisions are made to support special interest contributors' short-term profits ignoring the consequences of the longer-term cost to the economy and resource availability.

One good example is the low price of fuel, which ignores the cost to maintain the transportation infrastructure. Does it make sense to encourage the sale of fossil fuels when all of the experts recognize that this resource is limited? The only disagreement is just how much time remains before exhausting this resource. Would longer-term thinking dictate that higher fuel taxes with proceeds dedicated to infrastructure and alternative energy sources make more sense?

Another example is the out of control Federal spending that tends to satisfy current political agendas but which mortgages the future for many future generations. The facts are that our internal population is both aging and declining. Our total population continues to grow slightly via immigration, but our workforce continues to decline even with the addition of folks from other countries (both documented & undocumented). The decline means there are fewer workers to pay taxes to support spending, especially as it relates to Social Security & Medicare. The fact that healthcare costs have accelerated out of control, and many times faster than wages, adds to the problem. Average wages have only increased slightly since 2000, from $30,756 to $33,229 or less than 9%. For that same period, the median cost of a new house has increased from $165,814 to $315,815, or over 95%. During that same period, the cost of healthcare and advanced education has almost tripled! We started mortgaging the future several decades ago, and we are already experiencing the results.

There are many other examples, but one of the most recent was the tax reduction of 2017. It was deficit funded and is currently adding $150 Billion of red ink every year and will continue to do so for the next ten years. Not only will future generations have to pay the price, but the middle class did not receive their fair share of this redistribution of income. Our National Debt reached $23 trillion in November 2019. **Currently, we are adding $1 million to our debt every 35 seconds!** Two years ago, we were running an annualized deficit of approximately $800 Billion. Today (2019) it is running $1,036 Billion. Believe it or not, that is the good news. The level of unfunded liabilities for all the budget area commitments now **exceeds $125 trillion**. These are future costs that we have committed to pay but which we have not identified any revenues to support them. The unfunded liability for just one item, Medicare, exceeds $30 trillion.

I encourage readers to monitor the National Debt Clock: https://www.usdebt-clock.org/

CHAPTER 10:

Government Spending
& Transparency

The average voter is unaware of federal spending that is approved by their elected officials. We take debt for granted. We don't see it, and it doesn't appear on <u>our personal</u> financial statements. What can we use to measure debt levels? How can we determine if the level is reasonable?

The following shows the history of debt since 1980. Pay particular attention to the last column, Debt to GDP (<u>G</u>ross <u>D</u>omestic <u>P</u>roduct) ratio. This column is a decent indicator of our ability to service the debt. That ratio has increased by 300+ % since 1980. An argument is that interest rates are at an all-time low so we can afford to bear more debt. On average, we are only paying about 1.7% interest to service the debt. It is doubtful if this artificial level will exist <u>for the long- term.</u>

USA History of National debt since 1980

year	President	Debt added	Total debt	% increase	Debt to GDP Ratio
1980	James Earl Carter	$81,182,000,000	$907,701,000,000	9.8%	32%
1981	Ronald Wilson Reagan	$90,154,000,000	$997,855,000,000	9.9%	31%
1982	Ronald Wilson Reagan	$144,179,000,000	$1,142,034,000,000	14.4%	34%
1983	Ronald Wilson Reagan	$235,176,000,000	$1,377,210,000,000	20.6%	37%
1984	Ronald Wilson Reagan	$195,056,000,000	$1,572,266,000,000	14.2%	38%
1985	Ronald Wilson Reagan	$250,837,000,000	$1,823,103,000,000	16.0%	42%
1986	Ronald Wilson Reagan	$302,199,616,658	$2,125,302,616,658	16.6%	46%
1987	Ronald Wilson Reagan	$224,974,274,295	$2,350,276,890,953	10.6%	48%
1988	Ronald Wilson Reagan	$252,060,821,088	$2,602,337,712,041	10.7%	49%

1989	George Herbert Walker Bush	$255,093,248,146	$2,857,430,960,187	9.8%	50%
1990	George Herbert Walker Bush	$375,882,491,590	$3,233,313,451,777	13.2%	54%
1991	George Herbert Walker Bush	$431,989,899,920	$3,665,303,351,697	13.4%	59%
1992	George Herbert Walker Bush	$399,317,303,825	$4,064,620,655,522	10.9%	62%
1993	William Jefferson Clinton	$346,868,227,618	$4,411,488,883,139	8.5%	64%
1994	William Jefferson Clinton	$281,261,026,874	$4,692,749,910,013	6.4%	64%
1995	William Jefferson Clinton	$281,232,990,696	$4,973,982,900,709	6.0%	65%
1996	William Jefferson Clinton	$250,828,038,426	$5,224,810,939,136	5.0%	64%
1997	William Jefferson Clinton	$188,335,072,262	$5,413,146,011,397	3.6%	62%
1998	William Jefferson Clinton	$113,046,997,500	$5,526,193,008,898	2.1%	61%

1999	William Jefferson Clinton	$130,077,892,718	$5,656,270,901,615	2.4%	58%
2000	William Jefferson Clinton	$17,907,308,271	$5,674,178,209,887	0.3%	55%
2001	George Walker Bush	$133,285,202,313	$5,807,463,412,200	2.3%	55%
2002	George Walker Bush	$420,772,553,397	$6,228,235,965,597	7.2%	57%
2003	George Walker Bush	$554,995,097,146	$6,783,231,062,744	8.9%	59%
2004	George Walker Bush	$595,821,633,587	$7,379,052,696,330	8.8%	60%
2005	George Walker Bush	$553,656,965,393	$7,932,709,661,724	7.5%	60%
2006	George Walker Bush	$574,264,237,492	$8,506,973,899,215	7.2%	61%
2007	George Walker Bush	$500,679,473,047	$9,007,653,372,262	5.9%	62%
2008	George Walker Bush	$1,017,071,524,650	$10,024,724,896,912	11.3%	68%
2009	Barack Hussein Obama	$1,885,104,106,599	$11,909,829,003,512	18.8%	83%

2010	Barack Hussein Obama	$1,651,794,027,380	$13,561,623,030,892	13.9%	90%
2011	Barack Hussein Obama	$1,228,717,297,665	$14,790,340,328,557	9.1%	95%
2012	Barack Hussein Obama	$1,275,901,078,829	$16,066,241,407,386	8.6%	99%
2013	Barack Hussein Obama	$671,942,119,311	$16,738,183,526,697	4.2%	99%
2014	Barack Hussein Obama	$1,085,887,854,037	$17,824,071,380,734	6.5%	101%
2015	Barack Hussein Obama	$326,546,285,751	$18,150,617,666,484	1.8%	99%
2016	Barack Hussein Obama	$1,241,086,361,183	$19,573,444,713,937	7.8%	104%
2017	Donald John Trump	$671,455,302,117	$20,244,900,016,054	3.4%	103%
2018	Donald John Trump	$1,362,048,367,493	$21,606,948,383,546	6.3%	105%

Source for above: http://www.polidiotic.com/by-the-numbers/us-national-debt-by-year/

When I was taking economics classes in college in the '60s, the two most recognized economists were John Maynard Keynes and Milton Friedman. For Friedman, the level of debt was not as important as the level of government spending. He would rather see a $1 trillion-dollar budget with a high level of debt than a $2 trillion-dollar balanced budget since that would mean a high tax rate. He was in favor of cutting taxes no matter the condition of the economy. Keynes's view was a bit different. He was more concerned with the level of spending as he was with deficits. He felt that deficits were used during downturns in the economy, but that they should be balanced out by surpluses during good times. He was comfortable with an ongoing debt but felt that it should never exceed a certain ratio of Debt to GDP. I seem to recall that he was not in favor of a ratio above 75%, but I could be mistaken.

My issue is that the Government is a business, and borrowing decisions should be transparent. When in senior management with several companies and looking at borrowing to pay for equipment or a project, we asked the question; would the "payback" on the investment be three years or less?" While I am strongly in favor of reducing spending, what I also advocate is telling the truth. I like the idea of reducing taxes, but not if we are simply going to borrow to fund the tax change.

If the middle class only reaps about 1/3 of the tax reduction benefit, then I want to know it up front.

CHAPTER 11:

Fair Wage Compensation

Following is a repeat of a paragraph from Chapter 4

"If a family had of four had to pay their share of this cost (healthcare), they would be facing almost $44,000 annually. Anything less than an income of $75,000 per annum will require some form of subsidy. Families need funds to provide for basic housing, food, transportation, clothing, repairs & maintenance, insurance & a modest contingency fund."

A family, with both adults working above the current minimum wage, can expect their income to be less than $42,000 per year. This wage will not provide the entitlements that we would expect for our citizens. If only one adult is working then.........!!

What about the average situation for an experienced worker? The current median annual wage is just over $33,000, only 10% above what it was almost 20 years ago! The median family income is approximately $62,000, only 8% above that number almost 20 years ago. How will these citizens have any discretionary income to enable them to participate in capitalism?

One suggestion is to get rid of all of the undocumented workers. Then it will substantially reduce the available labor force and increase the demand and wages will rise. Some see this as a "free market" solution, and I am a staunch "free marketer." I can accept that this is true, but is it the best solution?

Let's consider some of the facts: The size of the workforce today is about 157,000,000. The Center for Migration Studies (CMS) has issued a report with this conclusion, which reinforces the findings of a similar report released by the Pew Research Center in November 2018. According to CMS, the total number of undocumented immigrants in the United States has decreased by one million since 2010 and now stands at about 10.7 million. The math says that undocumented workers represent about 6.8% of the current workforce. Will this reduction in the workforce yield more than a 7% rise in wages? I doubt it, and that amount of increase will not solve the problem.

The fact is that we do not have the workers to replace these folks. Why not? Other than immigration, our population is aging and declining. As a result, the availability of citizen workers is declining while the demand for workers is on the increase. I'm not advocating complete amnesty for our undocumented workers. We need to come up with a workable process where they can apply for residency while continuing to stay in our country. We also need a way for these folks to register and a way to identify those that are being protected by employers.

If we want to stop the flow of undocumented workers, then we need to en-force the laws that are already in place. Officials are fully aware of the compa-nies that are hiring undocumented workers (who in many cases are assisting them with false identities). If you have a problem, the best solution is to work upstream and identify the "cause" of the problem. Companies actively market to this labor group. Also, immigrants are fully aware of how to "game" our system. There is a legal process that allows immigrants the right to come into our country on a seasonal visa. Others come in on tourist visas. There is not an effective process to track these people after their temporary visas expire. They are well aware of which companies are willing to hire them on a more permanent basis. It is a fallacy to assume that the majority of the undocument-ed enter our country by illegally crossing our Southern Border.

My point is that we will not resolve the issue by deporting all of the undocumented workers.

If (or when) wages are improved enough to allow the average worker participation in capitalism who and how will the increase be funded? I guess that there will be a short-term price to be paid in terms of higher prices and a slowing of the economy. However, I see significant long-term benefits to our society in the form of providing a living wage with enough discretionary income to participate in capitalism.

CHAPTER 12:

Middle-Class Fairness

How big is the middle class, and how is it defined? *"The Pew Research Center defines the high end of the US middle class as those earning two-thirds to twice the median household income, which was $60,336 in 2017, meaning middle-class Americans were earning **about $40,425 to $120,672"** This group represents about 50% of the families in the U.S. "*

"A new survey by Northwestern Mutual found that 70 percent of Americans consider themselves middle class. However, a 2015 report from Pew Research Center shows that the middle class has been shrinking over the past four decades and now makes up only 50 percent of the United States' total population. One reason for this discrepancy might be the fact that wages have been largely flat while costs have gone up, so, in many places, even those making a six-figure income feel like they're struggling to get by.

Of the survey participants who labeled themselves as middle class, 50 percent earn between $50,000 and $125,000 annually. Although these Americans consider themselves in the middle, the actual dollar amounts needed to qualify as middle class are slightly lower. Pew Research Center defines the range as adults whose annual household income is two-thirds to double the national median, which was $55,775 as of 2016. This would lower the range to $40 to $110,000 That equates to singles making between $24,000 and $72,000 annually are middle class."

While the top 10% of income families have enough discretionary income to have some participation in Capitalism, it is the top 1% (the Capitalist Group) that controls wealth. The majority of middle-class families struggle to provide just one annual vacation. We can expect them to have little or no participation as owners of capital. Fully 37% of families have incomes below the definition of the middle class, and another 12% have incomes below the poverty level.

In the previous chapter, we reviewed the lower-income issue. We will also consider more in the next chapter. Currently, the middle class is the engine that drives our economy. Has this group been benefiting from the economic prosperity of the past 20 years? While GDP has increased from $9.6 trillion to $21.3 trillion (a 120% increase), average wages have only increased by about 10%. Where did all that additional GDP go?

CHAPTER 13

Citizens in Need of Assistance

There seems to be a lot of misinformation regarding this topic. Most of the funding for this area is listed under the broad heading of "income security." The major components of this budget item (currently just under $300 Billion annually) are Disability and financial assistance to families with very low or no income. I have had trouble verifying the breakdown, but doing the math on the number of persons receiving disability a conservative estimate is that it represents 40% of the total. Assuming this is close, that would mean about $180 Billion is going to what I used to refer to as "Welfare" payments or about 4% of the annual budget. Currently, about 40% of our citizens have incomes that are considered low (below middle class), and 12 – 14% are below the poverty line!

"Each year the Census Bureau uses poverty thresholds that are used for making overall calculations about the United States' population. This would include how many people are living in poverty. The Department of Health and Human Services uses a simplified version of the poverty thresholds, called poverty guidelines, which are used to determine whether families are eligible for federal entitlement programs, like food stamps, cash assistance, and social security. A family in poverty may qualify for more assistance than people who earn low incomes. A set of poverty guidelines applies to the 48 contiguous states. Hawaii and Alaska each have separate schedules. The guidelines are also updated annually. The official poverty guidelines for 2010 state that an annual income of $22,050 for a family of four lives at the poverty line. An

annual income of $44,100or below for that family of four would be considered low-income." These amounts have increased significantly since 2010.

Should we be assisting persons that are disabled and families with very low or no income? Absolutely. However, I have a couple of concerns:

First, I have issues with the way we monitor disability. My experience is that many people have disabilities that are not permanent, but our system allows some of these individuals to "game" the system. Others are working for cash and not reporting this income and this is cheating the taxpayer. Also, I think there should be a limited term for many disabled persons. The exception would be for those that are completely and permanently disabled. All subsidy recipients should be making a productive contribution to the country, even if it is only in an administrative capacity.

Next, I would point out that we currently subsidize low- and no-income families, and I would argue that we should continue to do so. I would also argue that an increase in wages, especially an increase in the minimum wage, would reduce the subsidy required to be funded by the taxpayers. As with the disability issue, I think that all persons and families receiving taxpayer-funded subsidies should be required to contribute in some meaningful form to the Country. I think that JFK got it right and understood the concept of self-worth-respect. *"Ask not what your country can do for you, but ask what you can do for your country."* I would add, *"if you are in need and feel you must ask for assistance, then also ask what you can contribute in return."*

CHAPTER 14:

The Best Representation that Money can Buy

While money is not the only factor that determines who gets elected, it is arguably the most significant. There are current restrictions on large single contributions, but there are several ways around this provision.

Source for the following: https://curiousmatic.com/ what-are-super-pacs-and-how-do-they-affect-elections/

Super PACs Basics

"Super PACs (Political Action Committees) were born in 2010 when the U.S. Supreme Court ruled that corporations have the same speech rights as individuals. The court's controversial decision effectively nullified The Tillman Act, which regulated political contributions in the U.S. for 107 years.

Super PACs exist only in the U.S., where they:

- ***Can raise unlimited sums from corporations, unions, and individuals***
- *Are controlled by independent committees- not the politicians who are*

running for office
- *Spend their money buying ads to advocate or attack candidates or build support for political positions"*

Who Runs Super PACs And How Much Money Is Donated?

"There are about 2,300 super PACs in the U.S., supporting various conservative and liberal political causes.

*The total money raised in 2016 (July figures) by the organizations was **over $940 million**, according to the non-profit watchdog Open Secrets.*

- ***Almost half of their funds*** <u>come from just 50 donors</u>
- *Of the top 10 organizations, around $320 million went to conservative organizations, while a little more than $130 million going to liberal ones*
- *Donors who champion specific industries often contribute. For instance, in 2015 <u>$62 million associated with fossil fuel supporters</u> flowed into similarly-aligned PACs*

Super PACs must be registered with the Federal Election Commission, and can only take money donated by U.S. entities or residents. They are run by committees that are responsible for their operations, and some are criticized for lack of transparency about their donors and richly rewarding committee members.

Super PACs are also criticized by advocates of election reform, who argue that the organizations pervert the electoral process and give large "mega-donors" unfair influence in elections."

How Do Super PACs Spend Their Money?

"The majority of Super PAC money goes to advertising, including:

- *Ads that support specific candidates and issues*
- *Attack ads that target opponents*

Though they can't donate directly to any one candidate, **the organizations have a limitless capacity to fund the way that any given candidate is packaged, advertised, and sold to voters."**

Another technique that corporations can employ was described to me by a friend that worked for a large wholesale distributor. The top executives and managers were invited to an "important" meeting. Managers learned they would be receiving a "special" bonus of $5,000 each (at the time the annual limit on a donation to a political party). They would also receive an additional amount to ensure that they could cover any additional tax liability (known as "grossing up"). They were also instructed to sign agreements so that the company could make the donations, individually, on behalf of each employee. It does not matter which party this was for (in this example it was in support of the Republican Party) as it is illegal regardless.

In part two of this book, I will suggest solutions that will lessen the impact of money in determining election outcomes.

CHAPTER 15:

Least Government is
the best Government

I have observed that very larger organizations become less productive the larger they are unless they break up their operations into smaller workgroups. And allow them some regulation and decision-making authority. It is not my intention to discuss this in-depth in this little book. You can accept my assertion or not. Larger companies can centralize certain administrative functions and benefit financially through an economy of scale. Size gives companies a market place advantage. However, if they do not decentralize operational areas, then creativity and productivity suffer, and these conditions tip in favor of smaller firms. Our Federal Government is huge and highly regimented. It is larger than any single firm in the private sector. Current expenditures (2019 actual, not "official") exceed $4.7 trillion and represent about 25% of GDP. Note that when the Government spends more, it increases GDP. Source: https://www.usdebtclock.org/

Productivity is poor, and creativity is not encouraged. Creativity can get you fired (if that is even possible as a "civil servant"). The Civil Service is the 2nd largest union in our country, just a bit smaller than the NEA (National Education Assoc.). We have many dedicated government workers handicapped by an inefficient and bureaucratic system. Also (and I dread saying this) they are overpaid when compared to comparable private-sector positions.

Currently, there are just under 3 million civil service employees, who represent almost 20% of all union workers. Nineteen percent of federal employees earned salaries of $100,000 or more in 2009. The average federal worker's pay was $71,208 compared with $40,331 for comparable positions in the private sector, according to the Office of Management and Budget. In 2010, there were 82,034 workers, 3.9% of the Federal workforce, making more than $150,000 annually, compared to 7,240 in 2005!

Since government workers make so much more than workers in the private sector, one would hope that they make up the difference in productivity? Again, such thinking is misguided. The Bureau of Labor Statistics does track productivity, but one could argue that it is like the fox watching the hen house. Bureau stats show a very slight annual increase in overall productivity per person (about 1% per year for the last 30 years or so). But a significant decrease in productivity per wages since they have increased at a much faster rate. There is one very significant issue with their stats, and that is the assumption that the baseline against which all future numbers was a reasonably productive number. And if you believe that then.......

CHART 2

Government Employees Work About One Month Less

Over the course of a calendar year, federal, state, and local government employees work about one month less than private-sector employees.

	Average Hours Worked in One Year	Hours, Compared to Private Sector	40-Hour Work Weeks, Compared to Private Sector
Private Sector	2,083	—	—
Federal Employees	1,930	153 fewer	3.8 fewer
State and Local Employees	1,896	187 fewer	4.7 fewer

Source: Author's calculations based on data from the U.S. Department of Labor, Bureau of Labor Statistics, American Time Use Survey, 2003–2010, http://www.bls.gov/tus/ (accessed August 31, 2012).

B 2724 ☎ heritage.org

The above chart is revealing, but it still does not address the issue of the productivity of the individual in the workplace. What it does reflect is that government workers make 75%+ more than private-sector workers and work 10% fewer hours.

Productivity is a very difficult item on which to find valid information, so I speculate a bit. I would be willing to bet all of the money in my bank account that a 10%+ improvement in individual productivity among all government workers is achievable. I suspect this expectation is too low. Achieving this result will never occur through any inspection or evaluation by an existing government agency.

Increasing productivity is possible, but not without significant changes in how the government is managed and structured. There is one significant area that has the potential to reduce spending, and that is Medicare & Medicaid. That area of our government represents over 20% of spending, and that has the potential to be cut in half. Please refer to more detail on this in Chapter 4.

To summarize, the factors of focus to reduce the size of government are cost efficiency (savings), productivity, and wage equity.

CHAPTER 16:

The Election Process

As recognized in previous chapters, the publics' candidate choices are in large part determined by money and the influence that it buys. Current restrictions were steps in the right direction, but they have been made ineffective by Super PACs and corporate abuses. Source for the following: https://www.washingtonpost.com/news/wonk/wp/2017/04/14/somebody-just-put-a-price-tag-on-the-2016-election-its-a-doozy/

"The final price tag for the 2016 election is in: $6.5 billion for the presidential and congressional elections combined, according to campaign finance watchdog OpenSecrets.org. The presidential contest — primaries and all — accounts for $2.4 billion of that total. The other $4 billion or so went to congressional races. The tally includes spending by campaigns, party committees, and outside sources."

"A week ahead of the 2018 election day, $4.7 billion has already been spent as shown by the Center for Responsive Politics easily making this the most expensive midterm in history. The final estimate will be $5.2 billion."

70 – 85% (depending on the party) of campaign financing comes from either a small number of large amount contributors or from Political Action Committees. Special interest groups control PACs and, have a very targeted agenda. Their agenda often it is not one that benefits the common good.

Campaigning typically begins at least a year in advance and often two years for the office of President. Is this in the best interest of the public? Consider the term of a member of the House of Representatives who spends ½ of his or her time in office campaigning for re-election.

Our representatives have developed a very lucrative compensation package, which includes a substantial salary and numerous fringe benefits. They have continued to prosper even during downturns in the economy. After five years a representative is fully vested for a lifetime retirement package. What the founding fathers viewed as a part-time "service" to the country with a modicum of compensation has morphed into a career pathway to considerable personal wealth.

For a history of congressional salaries visit: http://en.wikipedia.org/wiki/Salaries_of_members_of_the_United_States_Congress

Following is from http://usgovinfo.about.com/od/uscongress/a/congresspay.htm

"From 1789 to 1855, members of Congress received only a per diem (daily payment) of $6.00 while in session."

Rank-and-File Members:

The current salary (2015) for rank-and-file members of the House and Senate is $174,000 per year."

Following is from http://en.wikipedia.org/wiki/Congressional_pension

***"Congressional pension is a pension made available to members of the United States Congress.** Members who participated in the congressional pension system are vested after five (5) years of service. A full pension is available to Members 62 years of age with 5 years of service; 50 years or older with 20 years of service; or 25 years of service at any age" "In 2002, the average pension payment* *ranged from $41,000 to $55,000. As of November 2014[update], senior Members of Congress who have been in office for at least 32 years can earn about $139,000 a year."*

I believe that many, if not most, of our elected federal representatives, enter their first term in office with the best of intentions. However, for most this becomes the first step in a long career in politics. I suspect that it only takes a matter of months for a savvy house member to realize that he or she will need party support to achieve reelection. That effort will need to commence well before the election date. I tend to generalize here, so I apologize. Not all members fall into this category. A few have such a tremendous level of local support that their reelection is virtually assured. Most also are aware that the source of campaign funds comes from a relatively few very large sources, whom we might consider investors, "investors" with special interests. It is no wonder that campaigning for political office commences so far in advance of the election date. Is it possible for our representatives to look out for the common good while their focus is on re-election?

The most important element of our election process is funding. While not always true, it is a fact that the candidate with the most campaign money usually is victorious. Unfortunately, the very folks that like it that way are the ones with the power to change it, short of a Constitutional Amendment.

In Parliamentary systems, fixed election dates are not typical. The campaign period is often restricted to a 3 – 4-month period after the official election announcement, and this is considered too lengthy by many other countries.

What's even worse is that an exceptional amount of time and money doesn't produce an engaging democratic process. The U.S. ranks near the bottom in terms of voter participation when compared with other developed nations. Issues like obstacles to voter registration and the ability to get to the polls without missing work contribute to strikingly low turnout in the world›s most powerful democracy. Here's a brief look at some practices in other democracies.

The longest campaign in Canadian history was ten weeks.

In the U.K., political parties can only spend $30 million in the year before an election.

In Germany, political parties release just one 90-second television ad.

In 2013, over two-thirds of income to Norway's political parties came from the government.

Voter registration is automatic and required in Sweden.

CHAPTER 17

Effective & Participative Capitalism

I am a proponent for Capitalism, free markets (worldwide), and the need to encourage participation in this system by the majority of our citizens. Capitalism is superior to most (if not all) of the alternatives. In most cases, our system wins the day concerning productivity. We exist in a global economy, and our government should encourage and support all of our companies to enable them to compete internationally. Source for the following: https://en.wikipedia.org/wiki/Capitalism

*"**Capitalism** is an economic system based on the private ownership of the means of production and their operation for profit. Characteristics central to capitalism include private property, capital accumulation, wage labor, voluntary exchange, a price system, and competitive markets. In a capitalist market economy, decision-making and investments are determined by every owner of wealth, property or production ability in financial and capital markets, whereas prices and the distribution of goods and services are mainly determined by competition in goods and services markets."*

To participate in Capitalism, you need to have either a nest egg (inheritance, win the lottery, or have a rich & generous friend) or have a substantial salary. If you do not qualify for one of the situations in brackets, then you still might be able to invest a small amount in the stock market. A large portion of the public do not qualify.

I believe in reward-based compensation. The most productive labor needs to be rewarded. I know that many folks were upset when the 2018 deficit-financed tax cut rewarded companies by lowering the corporate tax rate. I was not. I make a case for eliminating all corporate taxes or at least making them just a token amount. No tax for companies horrifies many readers.

How much revenue is provided by companies? Before the tax change corporations were contributing about 9% to the treasury annually and this dropped to about 7% after the change (Refer to the debt clock at: https://www.usdebt-clock.org/). The fact is that companies play all sorts of accounting games to minimize taxes. Also, the amount they contribute has never been a significant factor.

Eliminating corporate tax would in the short term create abuses. Some companies would retain the extra earnings, and some executives would receive even more benefits on top of their already insane compensation. In the longer term, the market would stabilize, and competition would create benefit to the stockholders. Dividends will increase, consumers will see more competitive pricing and wages will rise (especially as the labor market tightens). I like the longer-term view.

Finally, this change would give our corporations a competitive advantage in the global market place. And it would eliminate the time and expense that companies spend to minimize their tax obligations.

My view is that Capitalism has the best chance to be effective in the long term, but some adjustments will ensure its longevity. We should abandon the old paradigm of adversity between management and labor. As advocates of capitalism, we should be providing ways and means where our employees can participate in the system. The term Compassionate Capitalism is likely not that appropriate. Perhaps Participative Capitalism is more valid. Our workers deserve to be part of the system and decision process.

CHAPTER 18:

Taxes – who pays, who should and "hidden taxes."

I admit that I am a bit addicted to the National Debt Clock. While the growth of our debt is alarming and our unwillingness to manage it unconscionable that web page carries quite a bit of useful information. Anyone can access that information at https://www.usdebtclock.org/

- What this site contains that pertains to taxes is a general breakdown of the sources of the tax revenues: 51% comes from taxes reported on personal tax forms, 35% from payroll taxes. 7% from companies & 7% from misc. other sources. Before the recent tax code change, the company portion stood at 9%. Many were appalled by the redistribution of income. I am not since in the long-term, all costs eventually are reflected in consumer pricing and become, in effect, a regressive tax.
- I am much more concerned with the impact of taxation on the middle class. There are numerous financial definitions of income to describe the middle class. In 2013, Congress quoted its definition of a middle-class income during the fiscal cliff compromise. It said the middle class is anyone making less $400,000 or couples making less than $450,000. The upper limit is far too high for me and does not define a range (there is no lower boundary). In an earlier chapter a definition from a non-governmental source was $45 -$110,000, and since this represents

almost 50% of the population, it seems a more reasonable range.

- Family incomes above $300,000 represent only 1% of the population. Family incomes below $30,000 represent 50% of the population. By this definition, the middle class represents about 49%. Also using this definition, the middle class (the primary consuming class) bears 63% of the tax burden. The middle class should be paying no more than their fair share (no more than 49%). The rich should be paying the amount required to make up for the lack of lower and below poverty families to pay tax (currently at about 4%). This bottom group struggles to survive.

CHAPTER 19:

The Free Market Economy

A free market is not perfect, especially when ownership of capital is very concentrated. Even as an imperfect system it fosters creativity and productivity. Source for the following: https://www.investopedia.com/terms/f/freemarket.asp

"The free market is an economic system based on supply and demand with little or no government control. It is a summary description of all voluntary exchanges that take place in a given economic environment. Free markets are characterized by a spontaneous and decentralized order of arrangements through which individuals make economic decisions"

"While no pure free-market economies actually exist, and all markets are in some ways constrained, economists who measure the degree of freedom in markets have found a generally positive relationship between free markets and measures of economic well-being."

Protectionists will argue against advocating completely free trade globally as it would devastate certain internal businesses that would not be able to compete on pricing. Many developing countries have a wage advantage in the short term. Other fully developed countries have both a technological and availability of capital advantage. In the short term, the industries within countries would be required to shift to businesses where they can compete. In the longer term, the market will balance out. Countries with a wage advantage will prosper in some areas and, as a result, raise the overall standard of living for their citizens. In the longer term, they will eventually reach a wage parity.

The best example I have of this is Japan. Their economy was in real trouble after WW II. They had to start from scratch, and initially, they relied on low-cost consumer items (and initially also low quality) to restart their economy. Wages were very low, and despite quality issues, they developed a growing economy. They eventually turned to more durable goods. They migrated into automotive and motorcycle manufacturing (as an aside, with the help of William Edwards Deming after being rejected as a consultant by Detroit). Source for the following: https://en.wikipedia.org/wiki/W._Edwards_Deming

"William Edwards Deming was an American engineer, statistician, professor, author, lecturer, and management consultant. Educated initially as an electrical engineer and later specializing in mathematical physics, he helped develop the sampling techniques still used by the U.S. Department of the Census and the Bureau of Labor Statistics"

Over time, with Deming's assistance, they produced more durable machines and did quite a bit of damage to a market that we once dominated. Deming's techniques were key to increasing product quality.

The rest is history as the Japanese economy is quite diverse, and their current standard of living mirrors the US. Their average wage now exceeds the US. In the process, Detroit finally recognized Deming's counsel and partially rebounded. They produce a far superior product today as a result of competition.

CHAPTER 20

Growth for the Sake of Growth

It seems that the economic success of a country is determined almost solely by GDP. In our country, if GDP is rising by 2 ½ - 3% then the economy is on a roll. When China's GDP drops below a 5% increase, they are in trouble. The reason for different expectations is that we live in a mature industrial country, and China is still in the developmental stage.

As the world's population continues to grow, our inability to sustain resources has become a reality. Experts disagree on what population the earth can sustain in the long term. On the most optimistic side, it is 5 Billion, and we are already way past that. Technology and the resulting improved productivity mean that sustaining a larger population will be possible, but there is a limit. Currently, we are using up resources a rate that will result in conflict among countries.

As mentioned earlier, the US has a negative internal population growth rate, and our modest rate of growth (at .7% per annum) is a result of immigration. I view this as a positive trend for the Earth. Slowing the world's rate of population growth is essential to our long-term survival if we want to avoid even more military actions between countries.

Focus on increasing GDP as a measure of success is short term thinking. The faster the rate of growth, the faster we use up limited resources. I am proposing that per capita GDP is a better measure of success since it does not depend on growth for just growths sake. Capital tends to concentrate among the wealthy, so per capita GDP is not the only important measure.

Another important factor is the distribution of the proceeds of GDP to citizens. These two elements, in my view, are much better measures of success. I would add one additional factor to track and report, and that is the Quality of Life Index, which takes into account numerous factors.

I have reprinted the GDP per Capita chart from a previous chapter as a reminder of where we stand compared to a few other countries. After that chart there is one that compares equality of income distribution followed by the quality of life by country.

Source: International Monetary Fund World Economic Outlook March 2018

	Country	Per Capita GDP 2018
1	Luxembourg	$ 115,203
2	Macao SAR	$ 86,339
3	Switzerland	$ 85,157
4	Norway	$ 82,773
5	Iceland	$ 79,271
6	Ireland	$ 77,160
7	Qatar	$ 72,677
8	United States	$ 65,062
9	Singapore	$ 62,984
10	Denmark	$ 62,041
11	Australia	$ 57,204
12	Sweden	$ 54,135
13	Netherlands	$ 54,129
14	Austria	$ 52,474
15	San Marino	$ 51,029
16	Finland	$ 50,879

17	Hong Kong SAR	$ 50,567
18	Germany	$ 49,692
19	Canada	$ 48,601
20	Belgium	$ 47,532

Below is a chart showing the quality of Income distribution by country with the most equal at top.

Country	UN R/P		World Bank Gini [3]		CIA R/P [4]			CIA Gini [5]
	10% [6]	20% [7]	%	Year	10%	Year	%	Year
Armenia	8.0	5.0	32.4	2015	25.8	2004	30.3	2012
Australia	12.5	7.0	34.7	2010	12.7	1994	30.3	2008
Austria	6.9	4.4	30.5	2014	6.8	2004	26.3	2007
Belgium	8.2	4.2	28.1	2014	8.3	2000	25.9	2013 est.
Canada	9.4	6.2	34.0	2013	9.5	2000	32.1	2005
Czech Republic	5.2	3.7	25.9	2014	5.2	1996	24.9	2012
Denmark	8.1	4.0	28.5	2014	12.0	2000 est.	24.8	2011 est.
Finland	5.6	3.9	26.8	2014	5.7	2000	26.8	2008
France	9.1	5.2	32.3	2014	8.3	2004	30.1	2013
Germany	6.9	5.1	31.4	2013	6.9	2000	27.0	2006
Greece	10.2	7.1	35.8	2014	10.4	2000 est.	34.4	2013 est.
Iceland		3.6	25.6	2014			28.0	2006
Ireland	9.4	5.1	31.9	2014	9.4	2000	33.9	2010
Italy	11.6	6.6	34.7	2014	11.7	2000	31.9	2012 est.
Japan	4.5	5.4	32.1	2008	4.5	1993	37.9	2011
Netherlands	9.2	4.4	28.6	2017	9.2	1999	25.1	2013
Norway	6.1	4.1	26.8	2014	6.0	2000	26.8	2010
Spain	10.3	7.3	36.0	2017	10.2	2000	34.0	2011
Sweden	6.2	4.6	27.2	2014	6.2	2000	24.9	2013
Switzerland	9.0	5.2	32.5	2013	8.9	2000	28.7	2012 est.
United Kingdom	13.8	5.4	34.1	2014	13.6	1999	32.4	2012
United States	18.5	9.4	41.5	2016	14.0	2014 est.	47.0	2014

Below is a list, best at the top, of quality of Life in Developed Countries.

Rank	Country	Quality of Life Index	Purchasing Power Index	Safety Index	Health Care Index	Cost of Living Index	Property Price to Income Ratio	Traffic Commute Time Index	Pollution Index	Climate Index
1	Denmark	196.47	110.69	75.28	79.22	83.88	7.52	29.6	20.79	82.29
2	Switzerland	196.08	127.76	78.82	73.23	122.67	9.11	29.12	21.31	79.24
3	Finland	195.06	108.78	77.25	75.27	72.18	7.88	30.62	11.57	62.79
4	Australia	189.73	118.09	57.3	76.82	73.39	7.68	35.66	23.15	94.2
5	Iceland	188.12	92.03	76.85	65.66	97.22	6.41	19.49	15.65	68.81
6	Austria	187.82	89.88	76.77	79.46	72.15	10.64	25.41	21.78	80.36
7	Netherlands	186.41	98.04	71.46	75.63	75.22	7.52	29.42	27.34	87.56
8	Germany	184.3	111.99	65.4	73.58	66.57	9.42	30.39	28.42	82.8
9	New Zealand	183.07	97.59	59.11	73.71	73.01	8.51	30.72	23.49	95.46
10	Sweden	180.52	112.75	52.79	69.41	70.11	9.61	30.04	17.45	73.58
11	Norway	179.78	98	66.49	74.36	104.49	8.61	27.24	20.29	71.37
12	Estonia	178.27	76.75	77.83	68.49	50.99	9.07	25.49	19.88	64.28
13	United States	176.77	119.1	53.27	69.23	70.95	3.54	32.66	35.74	76.75

In summary, my view is that some combination of GDP per capita, income equality, and quality of life should be tracked, reported and represent true economic status.

CHAPTER 21

Career Politicians &
Their Compensation

According to Wikipedia from 1789 to 1815, members of Congress received only a per diem (daily payment) of $6.00 while in session.

The current salary (as of 2015) for rank-and-file members of the House and Senate is $174,000 per year for a regular first termer; certain positions are a bit higher. While this ranks in the top 2% of wage earners in the U.S., I am ok with this salary compensation. However, I contend that they should play by the same rules as other civil servants concerning benefits, perks, retirement, etc. Actually, in some regards, they do now, but not all. Of course, term limits would have an impact on potential retirement payments.

Where are the current abuses? Source: http://www.opposingviews.com/i/politics/do-nothing-congress-set-work-only-8-more-days-year-will-put-barely-2-days-week-2014

1. *"Congress was only in session for 126 days in 2014.*
2. *Staff schedulers oftentimes make reservations for members of Congress via dedicated phone lines that Delta and other major airlines have reportedly set up for Capitol Hill customers. Airlines also permit members to reserve seats on multiple flights but only pay for the trips they take.*

3. *Whenever lawmakers decide to show up for a flight, they are also guaranteed free parking at the two Washington-area airports, according to a spokesman for the Metropolitan Washington Airports Authority.*

Note: *Some progress has been made on this issue in recent years, so it seems to be moving in a better direction for the taxpayer. Probably the reason that any and all representatives become millionaires (even one-termers) is a combination of the information they are privy to as well as the status gained by their position in regards to future employment (usually with lobbyists) & speaking engagements."*

PART TWO

CHAPTER 22:

Amendments

The proposed ERA Amendment:

"Section 1. Equality of rights under the law shall not be denied or abridged by the United States or by any State on account of sex.

Section 2. The Congress shall have the power to enforce, by appropriate legislation, the provisions of this article.

Section 3. This amendment shall take effect two years after the date of ratification."

The amendment should have been ratified, but it fell three states short. There is the talk of resurrecting it, but it is doubtful if it would ever pass. The opponents' view is that passing the amendment would provide more power to "Rowe vs. Wade" and make it more difficult to overturn. Since all 15 of the states that failed to ratify are very solidly **"Red,"** it is very doubtful that any will change their stance.

The other possibility would be the process of calling a National Convention to determine the possibility of adding the amendment. This process requires that 2/3 ds of the state legislatures (34) call for the convention. It might have a better chance.

Regardless, the intent of the amendment seems clear to me and the rights of women to make abortion decisions is a completely separate issue. My personal views on abortion are not relevant, but I do view this topic as most difficult one. I am an advocate for all people to take responsibility for their decisions. In this case, that would include taking responsibility for preventing pregnancy. There are some cases (such as rape) where that decision is not possible. However, the day after pill is still an option. In cases when that option is also not available, then I lean in favor of extremely short-term abortions. I fully understand why many would disagree with my position.

One amendment that I think is essential to our future is one that would provide for congressional term limits and modifications to benefit entitlements. Congress could easily take care of this issue, but they do not seem to be inclined to pass the required law. A large majority of the voters would applaud one.

One idea on term limits, which seems reasonable would be a total of 10 years of combined service (adding both House & Senate terms). Also, it should consider increasing the house term to four years instead of the current two.

Another potential and important amendment would limit campaign terms and spending. The idea on this would be to limit all national campaigns for the executive and congressional branches to 120 days before an election and to eliminate Super PACS. Also, total spending would be capped at a level easily reached by any candidate. My thinking would be $2 million for a House seat, $5 million for a Senate seat and $50 million for president. These Caps would be for the entire campaign (primaries and general elections) and would level the playing field. Also, political lobbies should be restricted if not eliminated. I favor the latter, but at the very least there should be a reasonable cap on advertising and any other spending on behalf of special interest. I'm thinking no more than $1 million per annum. Any campaign spending on behalf of a candidate would count against the candidate CAP.

CHAPTER 23:

Regaining Individual Freedoms

Following is a reprint from an earlier chapter of the Four Freedoms from FDR:

* *"The first is freedom of speech and expression – everywhere in the world.*

**The second is freedom of every person to worship God in his own way – everywhere in the world.*

** The third is freedom from want – which, translated into world terms, means economic understandings which will secure to every nation a healthy peacetime life for its inhabitants - everywhere in the world.*

** The fourth is freedom from fear – which, translated into world terms, means a world-wide reduction of armaments to such a point and in such a thorough fashion that no nation will be in a position to commit an act of physical aggression against any neighbor - anywhere in the world."*

Overall our country does an extremely good job with the 1st freedom. We generally tolerate the freedom to express any opinion and even outright falsehoods. I draw the line with a speech that advocates violence, hate, and bigotry. These expressions violate the overall intent of our constitution. Is it ok to "express" the desire to violate the constitution, or is "action" required before the authorities take action? In all honesty, I'm not certain. I do advocate official investigation into those that express dangerous intent and in keeping them under observation.

Again, we do an ok on **the 2nd freedom**. The earliest immigrants were typically a variety of Christian sects, and they were seeking freedom to express their beliefs without fear. What a lot of people do not realize is that a large number of the founding fathers were Deists. *"Deism is the belief that a **higher being (like the Christian God) exists, but does not tell people what to do**. Deism says that people should rely on logic and reason, and not the traditions of a religion that is based on a holy book. People who follow deism are called deists. Deists believe that a higher power created the world."*

This freedom was never intended only to protect the Christian Faith. We do tolerate some other belief systems (like Buddhism, Hinduism, etc.). We tend to be much less tolerant of Muslims because of certain extremists that advocate violence. It is understandable, but it is not acceptable to assume that all Muslims advocate violence. Our founders intended to provide a haven for all belief systems as long as they do not infringe on the rights of others. We need to be more tolerant and willing to listen to and understand the beliefs of others.

The 3rd freedom is freedom from want, and this is one on which we are losing a grip. We still are relatively ok, but the trend is going in the wrong direction. The issue of stagnant income for the middle class and the inability of lower-income groups to secure necessities through government subsidy was documented in previous chapters. As our economy has grown less of the benefit has accrued to both the middle- and lower-income classes. The 2017 debt-financed tax reduction did further damage to income distribution.

The first step would be to repeal the tax reduction act. It should be replaced (I'm not opposed to reducing taxes) with one that puts a larger tax burden on the top 10% of earners. My idea would be to increase the rates on the top 10% and redistribute most of the benefit to the middle class and raise the 0% tax rate to at least the bare subsistence level.

The following chart shows three tax bracket columns. All show the Marginal tax rate, the income bracket & I have added the average actual rate for the bracket.

Marginal Tax Rate	Married Filing Jointly – 2019	Actual Average rate	Marginal Tax Rate	Married Filing Jointly – 2017	Actual Average rate	Marginal Tax Rate	Married Filing Jointly - 2021	Actual Average rate
10%	$0-$19,400	10%	10%	$0 to $18,650	10%	0%	$0 to $10,000	0%
12%	$19,401-$78,950	12%	15%	$18,650 to $75,900	14%	5%	$10,001 to $50,000	4%
22%	$78,951-$168,400	17%	25%	$75,900 to $153,100	18%	10%	$50,001 to $100,000	7%
24%	$168,401-$321,450	21%	28%	$153,100 to $233,350	21%	20%	$100,000 to $250,000	13%
32%	$321,451-$408,200	23%	33%	$233,350 to $416,700	26%	30%	$250,001 to $500,000	21%
35%	$408,201-$612,350	28%	35%	$416,700 to $470,700	28%	40%	$500,001 to $2,000,000	34%
37%	Over $612,350	29 - 35%	39.5%	above $470,700	30 - 38%	50%	above $2,000,001	35 - 45%

The column of brackets shows the data for 2019. The second is for 2017 (before the tax reduction), and the last shows **my idea** of what would be more equitable for the middle class, be much less costly to administer and still cost tax payers less than the 2019 plan.

The following chart is one I prefer and is based on **Gross Income levels** with few or no deductions:

Marginal Tax Rate	Married Filing Jointly – 2021 (New system)	Actual rate Average
0%	$0 to $25,000	0%
3%	$25,001 to $50,000	1.5%
5%	$50,001 to $100,000	3.5%
8%	$100,000 to $250,000	6%
15%	$250,001 to $500,000	11%
25%	$500,001 to $2,000,000	22%
35%	above $2,000,001	22 - 33%

Dependent exemptions would be limited to 2.

Also, I would propose an annual tax on wealth (assets minus liabilities). The proposed bracket rates would be: 0 % for under $5,000,000, .5% for $5,000,001 - $10,000,000, 1% for $10,000,001 to $50,000,000 and 1.5% for $5,000,001 to $100,000,000 and 2% over $100,000,001.

I would eliminate corporate income taxes.

Also, the Federal minimum wage needs to be adjusted as it applies to employees over the age of 18. I am ok with $15 per hour, but there should be a phase-in period for entry-level jobs. My idea on this is that entry-level & first-time jobs would start at $10 per hour, increase to $12.50 after a year, and reach the $15 minimum after two years.

The fourth freedom has to do with living in a safe and secure environment. The 3rd freedom must be in place first; otherwise, people are too busy trying to survive to worry about other issues. One view is that the way to provide security is through an aggressive military stance. While our ability to defend and respond to aggression is essential, it is even more important to form and nurture alliances with other countries. Indeed, some of our alliances are not completely fair concerning the financial burden. I favor negotiations to resolve these issues. If anything, we need to explore ways that we can strengthen relations with our allies. Also, we need to find areas of common ground with countries that we do not consider allies. A good example of this would be our relationship with North Korea.

North Korea is a family-run dictatorship, a concept that we abhor. They do not value human rights, and they are a potential nuclear threat. Their intention has and is still the unification of Korea under their rule. Is the way forward military posturing and exchanging missile testing for military exercises?

What we want are limits on North Korea's nuclear capabilities. We would also like a positive change in their position on human rights. Something they might want would be relief from trade restrictions and economic assistance. It might be possible to use what each side wants as a starting point for meaningful discussions. The best approach would be to start with a select team from each country meeting in a neutral location. Each side would take proposals back to their leadership, which would then result in a summit between the two leaders. It is unrealistic to expect quick results, but beginning the process is important, and maintaining a long-term dialogue can only improve relations.

We need to focus strictly on defense and the elimination of international terrorist organizations. We need to stay out of civil conflicts in other countries. We do not have the right or the money to serve as the world's cop.

CHAPTER 24:

The Importance of Leadership

"Great leaders find the balance between business foresight, performance, and character. They have vision, courage, integrity, humility, and focus along with the ability to plan strategically and catalyze cooperation amongst their team."

Vision

"Good business leaders create a vision, articulate the vision, passionately own the vision, and relentlessly drive it to completion." – Jack Welch

Great leaders have a vision… They can see into the future. They have a clear, exciting idea of where they are going and what they are trying to accomplish and are excellent at strategic planning.

Courage

"Courage is rightly considered the foremost of the virtues, for, upon it, all others depend." – Winston Churchill

One of the more important qualities of a good leader is courage. Having the quality of courage means that you are willing to take risks in the achievement of your goals with no assurance of success. Because there is no certainty in life or business, every commitment you make and every action you take entails a risk of some kind.

Integrity

"With integrity, you have nothing to fear, since you have nothing to hide. With integrity, you will do the right thing so that you will have no guilt." – Zig Ziglar

The core of integrity is truthfulness. Integrity requires that you always tell the truth, to all people, in every situation. Truthfulness is the foundation quality of the trust that is necessary for the success of any business.

Humility

Humility gets results. Larry Bossidy, the former CEO of Honeywell and author of the book Execution, explained why leadership characteristics, such as humility, make you a more effective leader:

"The more you can contain your ego, the more realistic you are about your problems. You learn how to listen, and admit that you don't know all the answers. You exhibit the attitude that you can learn from anyone at any time. Your pride doesn't get in the way of gathering the information you need to achieve the best results. It doesn't keep you from sharing the credit that needs to be shared. Humility allows you to acknowledge your mistakes." – Larry Bossidy

Great leaders are those who are strong and decisive but also humble.

Humility doesn't mean that you're weak or unsure of yourself. It means that you have the self-confidence and self-awareness to recognize the value of others without feeling threatened.

Humility is one of the rarer attributes – or traits – of good leaders because it requires containment of one's ego.

It means that you are willing to admit you could be wrong, that you recognize you may not have all the answers. And it means that you give credit where credit is due – – which many people struggle to do.

Strategic Planning

"Strategy is not the consequence of planning, but the opposite: it's the starting point." – Henry Mintzberg

Great leaders are outstanding at strategic planning. It's another one of the more important leadership strengths. They can look ahead, to anticipate with some accuracy where the industry and the markets are going.

Focus

"Successful people maintain a positive focus in life no matter what is going on around them. They stay focused on their past successes rather than their past failures, and on the next action steps, they need to take to get them closer to the fulfillment of their goals rather than all the other distractions that life presents to them. – Jack Canfield

Leaders always focus on the needs of the company and the situation. Leaders focus on results, on what must be achieved by themselves, by others, and by the company. Great leaders focus on strengths, in themselves and in others.

Cooperation

"If your imagination leads you to understand how quickly people grant your requests when those requests appeal to their self-interest, you can have practically anything you go after." – Napoleon Hill

Your ability to get everyone working and pulling together is essential to your success. Leadership is the ability to get people to work for you because they want to.

The <u>80/20 rule</u> applies here: Twenty percent of your people contribute to 80 percent of your results.

Your ability to select these people and then to work well with them daily is essential to the smooth functioning of the organization.

Gain the cooperation of others by getting along well with each key person every single day. You always have a choice when it comes to a task: You can do it yourself, or you can get someone else to do it for you. Which is it going to be?

If we want effective leadership in our elected representatives, we will do well to evaluate current and prospective politicians in light of the proceeding seven criteria.

CHAPTER 25:

Restoring Affordable Healthcare

In Part One, the topic of healthcare was by far the longest and most in-depth chapter. There was a valid reason for the detail. This topic is by far the most important to the future financial health of both the country and our citizens. **It is arguably as important as all of the other topics in this book combined.** For this reason, this chapter, which explores feasible solutions, will contain considerable detail.

Solving this issue will not only improve the affordability and quality of healthcare it will vastly improve the financial condition of our country. The solution is extremely simple to implement, but next to impossible to enact politically. Why not you ask? The reason is that there are too many powerful "special interests" that are making hundreds of billions **each** off the current system.

The simple solution is to evaluate other countries' systems that are providing superior quality of care at a much lower per capita cost. This process is called "baselining" The following chart show 5 of the top 10 countries in quality of care and their per capita cost.

Best Quality of Care Ranking	2012 Per Capita Cost
1 France	$3,974
2 Italy	$2,962
7 Spain	$3,076
9 Austria	$4,395
10 Japan	$3,035
37 USA	11,000
	(3.1 x top 10 average)

Average per capita cost of top 10 in quality $3,481

The procedure would be to have unbiased experts examine the systems of the five countries that rank in the top 10 on quality of care. And take the best of each that makes good sense and redesign our system from the ground up. It will be critical to use a team of "experts" that are independent of the following industries: The AMA, drug companies, health insurance companies, the legal profession, and hospitals. We need an unbiased view of all of these components of a healthcare system. I am not qualified to evaluate the systems of the "baseline" countries, but the following are top line summaries for each:

France: (Source: <u>https://about-france.com/health-care.htm</u>)

*"**The French health care system** is generally recognized as offering one of the best, services of public health care in the world. Above all, it is a system that works, provides universal cover, and is a system that is strongly defended by virtually everyone in France.*

The health care system in France is made up of a fully-integrated network of public hospitals, private hospitals, doctors and other medical service providers. It is a universal service providing health care for every citizen, irrespective of wealth, age or social status."

Italy: (Source: <u>https://healthmanagement.org/c/it/issuearticle/</u>
<u>facts-figures-the-italian-healthcare-system</u>)

"Italy has a national health plan (Servizio Sanitario Nazionale), which provides universal coverage for hospital and medical benefits, however about 30% of the population has contracted additional private health insurance. The Italian public healthcare system is decentralized and is based on three levels: the State, region and local health boards. The State is responsible for issuing general system guidelines, establishing work contracts, handling international relations and financing research hospitals. The 20 regions of Italy control the functioning of the health services within their areas of jurisdiction and finance independent hospitals. Finally, the local health-care units provide daily management of services and finance public and private hospitals under contract with the regions. The remaining private hospitals are financed by their patients."*

Spain: (Source: <u>https://healthmanagement.org/c/hospital/</u>
<u>issuearticle/overview-of-the-spanish-healthcare-system</u>)

"The Spanish National Healthcare System ("Instituto Nacional de la Salud"), founded in Spain's General Healthcare Act of 1986, guarantees universal coverage and free healthcare access to all Spanish nationals, regardless of economic situation or participation in the social security network.*

In 1998 the Sistema Sanitario Público (public health service) brought in an official mandate for both doctors and patients outlining the service to which they are entitled, explained in the Carta de Derechos y Deberes (Charter of Rights and Obligations).

Management: The national system has been decentralized since 2002, which has given the regional healthcare authorities the autonomy to plan, change and upgrade the infrastructure, leading to enormous development in the healthcare technology scenario, especially in the usage of information technology. The reforms, which regionalized the system, were implemented in order to provide greater and equal access to the population, thus avoiding the concentration of health services in urban areas. This has also improved response time and increased the participation of the target community in the development and management of the national healthcare system at regional and local levels."

Austria: (Source: https://en.wikipedia.org/wiki/ Healthcare_in_Austria)

"The nation of Austria has a two-tier health care system *in which virtually all individuals receive publicly funded care, but they also have the option to purchase supplementary private health insurance. Care involving private insurance plans (sometimes referred to as "comfort class" care) can include more flexible visiting hours and private rooms and doctors. Some individuals choose to completely pay for their care privately.*

Healthcare in Austria is universal for residents of Austria as well as those from other EU countries. Students from an EU/EEA country or Switzerland with national health insurance in their home country can use the European Health Insurance Card. Self-insured students have to pay an insurance fee of EUR 52.68 per month.

Enrollment in the public health care system is generally automatic and is linked to employment, however, insurance is also guaranteed to co-insured persons (i.e. spouses and dependents), pensioners, students, the disabled, and those receiving unemployment benefits. Enrollment is compulsory, and it is not possible to cross-shop the various social security institutions. Employers register their employees with the correct institution and deduct the health insurance tax from employees' salaries. Some people, such as the self-employed, are not automatically enrolled but are eligible to enroll in the public health insurance scheme. The cost of public insurance is based on income and is not related to individual medical history or risk factors.

All insured persons have issued an e-Card, which must be presented when visiting a doctor (however, some doctors only treat privately insured patients). The e-Card allows for the digitization of health claims and replaces the earlier health insurance voucher. Additionally, the e-Card serves as a valid ID.

Hospitals and clinics can be either state-run or privately run. Austria has a relatively high density of hospitals and physicians; In 2011 there were 4.7 Physicians per 1000 people, which is slightly greater than the average for Europe. In-patient care is emphasized within the Austrian healthcare system; Austria has the most acute care discharges per 100 inhabitants in Europe and the average hospital stay is 6.6 days compared with an EU average of 6."

Japan: (Source: <u>https://en.wikipedia.org/wiki/ Health_care_system_in_Japan</u>)

"The health care system in Japan *provides healthcare services, including screening examinations, prenatal care, and infectious disease control, with the patient accepting responsibility for 30% of these costs while the government pays the remaining 70%. Payment for personal medical services is offered by a universal health care insurance system that provides relative equality of access, with fees set by a government committee. All residents of Japan are required by the law to have health insurance coverage. People without insurance from employers can participate in a national health insurance program, administered by local governments. Patients are free to select physicians or facilities of their choice and cannot be denied coverage. Hospitals, by law, must be run as non-profit and be managed by physicians. For-profit corporations are not allowed to own or operate hospitals. Clinics must be owned and operated by physicians.*

Medical fees are strictly regulated by the government to keep them affordable. Depending on the family's income and the age of the insured, patients are responsible for paying 10%, 20%, or 30% of medical fees, with the government paying the remaining fee.[1] *Also, monthly thresholds are set for each household, again depending on income and age, and medical fees exceeding the threshold are waived or reimbursed by the government.*

Uninsured patients are responsible for paying 100% of their medical fees, but fees are waived for low-income households receiving a government subsidy. Fees are also waived for homeless people brought to the hospital by ambulance."

Changing the System will go a long way towards improving the quality of care, but it will only have a limited impact on costs. We need to examine each element of the costs involved. We need to determine why they are so much higher in our country when compared to the five countries in the baseline group (in the following chart I have substituted Germany for Austria since I could not find the exact comparison for Austria, but they should be about the same).

The Cost of Prescription Drugs

2017 Prescription Drug Cost Savings

The average percentage saved outside the U.S. for select prescriptions.

France 67%   Italy 53%   Spain 55%

Japan 65%   Germany 51%

One significant factor in the cost disparity is that the R & D costs by US pharmaceutical companies are borne via domestic pricing. Export sales are considered "incremental" and pricing is much, much lower.

"Hopkins University, tells NPR that raising the cost of existing drugs benefits drugmakers and insurers.

Research and development is only about 17 percent of total spending in most large drug companies," he says. "Once a drug has been approved by the FDA, there are minimal additional research and development costs so drug companies cannot justify price increases by claiming research and development costs.

The study did not examine why prices of existing drugs have gone up, but the researchers say a lack of competition and the regulatory environment in the U.S. allow "for price increases much higher than in other countries."

From 2008 through 2014, average prices for the most widely used brand-name drugs jumped 128%, according to prescription-benefit manager Express Scripts Holding Co. Reasons include increasing research costs, insufficient competition, and drug shortages.

However, none of these issues completely explain the price disparity. We do need some form of price controls, especially on "mature drugs" and also some assurance that R&D costs are factored into worldwide pricing. Also, we need to investigate the pricing in the baseline countries for the most consumed drugs. If there is a significant price difference, then the companies should be called before Congress to justify. Based on the data from the baseline countries, these costs should be reduced by 50% at a minimum.

Legal Factors in Healthcare Costs

We have nine times as many lawyers per capita as France and forty times as many as Japan. Does this make sense to you? Medical issues have become a staple for the Legal Industry. I am convinced that when there is an oversupply of lawyers, they have no choice to create additional business opportunities. The result is an increase in costs to drug companies and physicians and hospitals in the form of malpractice insurance.

One example that amazes me is the blood thinner drug Xarelto. As of this writing, they had settled a class-action lawsuit. I found the following describing the results of the suit.

"Makers of the powerful blood thinner Xarelto have agreed to pay $775 million to settle about 25,000 lawsuits that claim the drug caused serious injuries such as internal bleeding, stroke, and death. "It may have taken more than four years and six separate trials but litigation like this is an important way for consumers to have a voice in matters of drug safety," attorney Brian Barr, co-lead counsel for plaintiffs in the litigation, said in a news release.

Bayer and Johnson & Johnson jointly sell Xarelto and will each pay half of the settlement. Neither company admitted liability."

While this is not surprising, the fact that they are still aggressively advertising the drug on TV is!

I can't excuse the abuses of Drug companies outlined in Chapter 4. But there is clear evidence that the legal profession is one industry that is milking the healthcare system and thus the taxpayer.

Source for the following: https://en.wikipedia.org/wiki/
List_of_largest_pharmaceutical_settlements\

"The National Practitioner Data Bank, a computer database of the United States Department of Health and Human Services that collects information about physicians, has released its annual report concerning medical malpractice payouts. According to the published report, approximately $4,031,987,700 was paid to plaintiffs in medical malpractice lawsuits in 2018.

The following is a list of some of the largest settlements reached between the United States Department of Justice and pharmaceutical companies from 1991 to 2012, ordered by the size of the total settlement."

Year	Company	Settlement	Violation(s)	Product(s)	Laws allegedly violated (if applicable)
2012	GlaxoSmithKline[1][6]	$3 billion ($1B criminal, $2B civil)	Criminal: Off-label promotion, failure to disclose safety data. Civil: paying kickbacks to physicians, making false and misleading statements concerning the safety of Avandia, reporting false best prices and underpaying rebates owed under the Medicaid Drug Rebate Program	Avandia (not providing safety data), Wellbutrin, Paxil (promotion of paediatric use), Advair, Lamictal, Zofran, Imitrex, Lotronex, Flovent, Valtrex;	False Claims Act/FDCA
2009	Pfizer[2]	$2.3 billion	Off-label promotion/kickbacks	Bextra/Geodon/Zyvox/Lyrica	False Claims Act/FDCA
2013	Johnson & Johnson[7]	$2.2 billion	Off-label promotion/kickbacks	Risperdal/Invega/Nesiritide	False Claims Act/FDCA
2012	Abbott Laboratories[8]	$1.5 billion	Off-label promotion	Depakote	False Claims Act/FDCA
2009	Eli Lilly[9]	$1.4 billion	Off-label promotion	Zyprexa	False Claims Act/FDCA
2001	TAP Pharmaceutical Products[10]	$875 million	Medicare fraud/kickbacks	Lupron	False Claims Act/ Prescription Drug Marketing Act
2012	Amgen[11]	$762 million	Off-label promotion/kickbacks	Aranesp	False Claims Act/FDCA
2010	GlaxoSmithKline[12]	$750 million	Poor manufacturing practices	Kytril/Bactroban/Paxil CR/Avandamet	False Claims Act/FDCA
2005	Serono[13]	$704 million	Off-label promotion/kickbacks/monopoly practices	Serostim	False Claims Act

The Largest drug-related class action settlement was in 2000

"Fen-Phen diet drugs $3.8 billion

In 2000, a federal judge in Philadelphia approved a $3.75 billion settlement over a diet drug known as fen-phen that had been associated with potentially fatal heart valve damage. Six million people reportedly used fen-phen, sold by American Home Products, before it was pulled from the market in 1997. The settlement provides up to $1.5 million to users, depending on their injuries and how long they used the drug."

"News flash, just announced by far the largest settlement offer to date and this is for only one drug and one company involved in the Opioid Crisis:

The maker of OxyContin, Purdue Pharma, and its owners, the Sackler family, are offering to settle more than 2,000 lawsuits against the company for $10 billion to $12 billion. The potential deal was part of confidential conversations and discussed by Purdue's lawyers at a meeting in Cleveland last Tuesday, Aug. 20, (2019), according to two people familiar with the mediation.

Brought by states, cities, and counties, the lawsuits — some of which have been combined into one m massive case — allege the company and the Sackler family are responsible for starting and sustaining the opioid crisis."

Additional Update: In November 2019 it was announced that the current offer to settle the Opioid Class action was now at $50 Billion for the two largest manufacturers of the product!

The point is that in the long run all of these costs end up being passed along to the consumer in the form of higher prices (you might say an added tax).

Physician Fees

U.S. physicians are the best paid in the world. It is also true that the cost of their education is also the highest in the world, but that is a subject for another day. The cost of malpractice insurance is also a factor. It is not unusual for a physician to be facing a student loan debt of $500,000 when they begin their practice or job. However, at an average annual income approaching $250,000 (the average for GPs, Specialists, and Surgeons) their repayment ability far exceeds most other professions. Why is there a large variance in compensation when compared to our baseline countries?

Source for the following: https://content.wisestep.com/ highest-paying-countries-doctors/

*"Many believe that **the USA** pays the most to its Doctors. However, the USA is in the number three position. A specialist (non-surgeon) in the USA makes around $230,000 annually, whereas a general practitioner goes home with a $161,000 roughly."*

In Japan, *the best data I could locate was that the average GP makes about $140,000 per year."*

*"**In France**, there is a pharmacy in almost every corner of the street. Specialists here earn approximately an average of $149,000 and GP`s roughly earn $92,000 annually."*

*"**In Spain,** a person working in Doctor / Physician in Spain typically earns around 7,292 EUR per month. This is the average monthly salary, including housing, transport, and other benefits."*

*"**In Norway,** a Doctor can expect to earn a decent amount, nothing that fancies though. Specialists make around $77,000, while general practitioners earn approximately $66,000."*

*"**In Austria,** The gross annual income for doctors in their first year practicing is about 50,000€. You reach about 60,000€ in the fourth year usually."*

The physician compensation in all of the baseline countries is considerably lower than in the U.S. The AMA will not be happy with me, but I do not think that providing health care should be viewed as a for-profit business. I also think that making a career decision to serve the public should not come with it a large educational debt. I would recommend that we study the physician compensation methods of the baseline countries. And make changes that will phase-in both wage standards and education subsidies for our doctors.

Hospital Costs (source: <u>https://worldofdtcmarketing.com/ hospital-care-is-the-largest-driver-of-u-s-health-prices/</u>)

"Total health care spending in America was approximately $3.5-trillion in 2017, and about 32% of that amount — or $1.1-trillion — is spent on hospital services."

Hospitals are an area where our costs are completely out of whack! I have no idea why we are so out of line with the other countries.

There are numerous documented examples of hospital financial abuse in this country. Overcharges for OTC medications, overprescribed testing, and phantom charges are among these examples. In the U.S. we pay more for hospital services than in all other countries. Do we receive superior care in exchange? Considering where we rank in terms of quality of care, it is doubtful.

This area cries out for some serious baselining. I have not been able to locate the cost of a hospital day for all of the baseline countries. But there is little doubt that they all have a lower per day cost than the U.S.

I am reprinting the chart below from Chapter 4 again to illustrate the issue. It contains the numbers for a couple of the baseline countries, France and Spain.

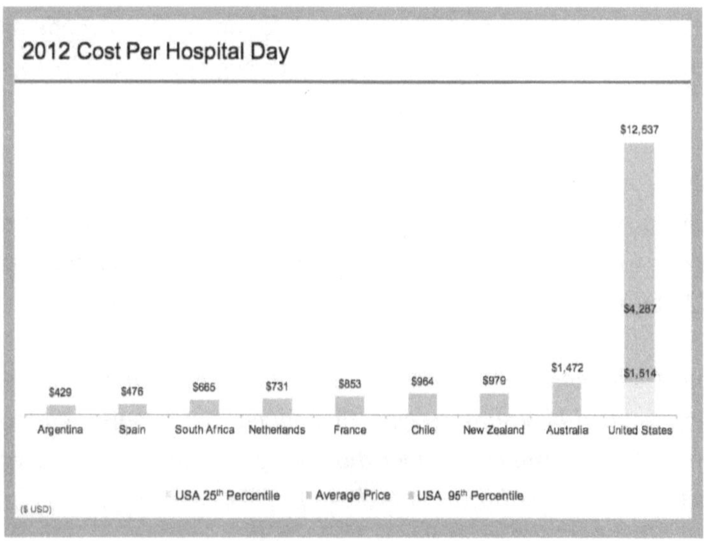

Insurance Companies

I am not convinced that putting a middle man into providing health care makes much sense? If they can do it more efficiently, it does, but the facts are disturbing as you can see from the following:

Health Care Premiums Also Used for Lavish Salaries, Luxury Items, Underwriters

Nov. 3, 2009, By KATE SNOW, ELIZABETH TRIBOLET and SUZAN CLARKE via

"A significant portion of health insurance premiums goes not for actual medical care but for private jets, generous CEO salaries, and underwriters who decide when to drop patients who become too expensive, according to a Senate committee report.

Sen. John D. Rockefeller, D-W.Va., chairman of the Senate Committee on Commerce, Science and Transportation, wrote to 15 of the biggest health insurance companies in August, asking them to provide information on how much of policyholders' monthly premiums was spent on medical care versus the amount that went to administrative costs and company earnings.

Such figures are known in the insurance industry-speak as "medical loss ratios." But when insurance companies balked, saying the information was confidential and proprietary, Rockefeller's investigators went digging through public documents and found that much of policyholder premiums were going to nonmedical costs.

The insurance industry has long pointed to federal data that says about 87 percent of every dollar that people spend on premiums goes toward actual medical care, but Rockefeller's investigators found the average for the top six insurance companies is closer to 82 cents on the dollar for medical care.

That five-point difference represents billions of dollars. And when investigators broke down the information by insurance type, they found that people who buy individual insurance from those companies rather than being part of a small or large business, get the least bang for their buck. On average just 74 cents of every premium dollar for individual coverage goes to medical care. Coventry Health Care had the lowest figure at 66 cents"

I suspect the health insurance companies are excited by the Affordable Care Act. Now all of us <u>must</u> have health insurance, and we pay the penalty if we refuse! We are better off taking the middleman completely out of the process.

That said, I am not in favor of completely decimating private medical insurance as long as they can provide comparable and competitively priced services. The fact that Medicare's administrative costs run less than 2%. The average costs and profits for insurance companies at 26% is telling.

How are the baseline countries handling health insurance? I am confident that an efficient system similar, to one already in place in another country, can be implemented by us.

Health Education

As was pointed out in chapter four, we spend about $8 billion a year on health education and yet average health in our country is not improving. Obesity & overweight continues to increase, and longevity is decreasing despite our best efforts to extend life (we currently rank 57th in projected longevity). It is not unusual that a person's medical cost will be more in the last year of life than all of the preceding years combined.

The key to health is the condition of the immune system. Admittedly, there are hereditary factors that predetermine certain events, but even in these instances, longevity will improve with a high functioning immune system.

Defenders of the current health education program claim that the condition would be even worse if we abandon education.

I am not proposing that we abandon efforts to improve health, just that we refocus our efforts and reduce spending. I would eliminate spending at the

Federal level and Cap the overall spending at $4 billion. I would push the spending down to the community level. Communities could apply for grants that require 1/3 local funding (in-kind services allowed) which would be limited to a maximum of $5 per capita per year (a city of 50,000 could apply for a maximum annual grant of $250,000. The proposals must contain both exercise and healthy eating components. The maximum duration for any grant proposal would be three years. After that, the community would be expected to maintain and fund the effort locally.

I would also aggressively address the obesity issue in two ways. There would be a phase-in period of 3 years. Persons that are currently obese would be given three years to reduce their BMI to 32 or below. Source: https://www.medicinenet.com/script/main/art.asp?articlekey=11760

*"BMI (Body Mass Index) of 30 and above. (A BMI of 30 is about **30 pounds overweight**.) The BMI, a key index for relating body weight to height, is a person's weight in kilograms (kg) divided by their height in meters (m) squared."*

The only exception would be in the rare cases where obesity is a result of a medical condition or disability, and in all those cases would require a physician certification. There would be heavy financial penalties for false or forged certifications. Obese persons who bring their BMI to under 32 in the 1st year would receive a $1,000 tax credit in year two and year 3. Those that achieve the goal in year two would receive the credit in year 3. Commencing in year four all persons with a BMI of 32 or over would be subject to a $500 annual Income tax penalty. The penalty would apply to each obese person in the household. Further, obese persons would not be eligible for any federal government subsidies such as food stamps (EBTs).

The single most effective activity for improving and maintaining the immune system is an effective exercise regimen. What you consume is important, but exercise is the key. An effective exercise program involves a minimum of 30 minutes a day that includes elevating the heart rate to at least 50% above the at-rest rate. Example: if your at-rest rate is 60 bpm then ensure that your exercise rate is at least 90 bpm. For the average person, this would mean brisk walking at about 3.5 mph. You can easily gauge your walking speed by the distance covered in 30 minutes which would be 7/8 mile (1,400 meters) at 3.5 mph. This rate of speed will likely not be possible for many obese persons, but it is one that is attainable in less than 30 consecutive days of walking. This routine will easily take a person with a BMI of 35 to below 32 in less than six months as long as their caloric intake does not increase. Walking is free; it only requires time. My favorite reference on this topic is a video called 23 ½ hours at https://www.youtube.com/watch?v=aUaInS6HIGo.

Relative Quality of Life

More important than longevity is the length of time that we experience "quality" life experience. The following chart again shows how we compare to other countries.

Following was taken from http://en.wikipedia.org/wiki/
List_of_countries_by_life_expectancy

- HEALTHY LIFE EXPECTANCY (HALE)

Health attainment, level, and distribution in all Member States

Disability-adjusted life expectancy at birth (years) Adjusted for years spent in disability. When compared to longevity, the chart is revealing. It indicates that the last ten years of life are not pleasant (on average) and also likely very expensive.

Rank	Country	Total	Male	Female
1	Japan	74.5	71.9	77.2
2	Australia	73.2	70.8	75.5
3	France	73.1	69.3	76.9
4	Sweden	73.0	71.2	74.9

5	Spain	72.8	69.8	75.7
6	Italy	72.7	70.0	75.4
7	Greece	72.5	70.5	74.6
8	Switzerland	72.5	69.5	75.5
9	Monaco	72.4	68.5	76.3
10	Andorra	72.3	69.3	75.2
11	San Marino	72.3	69.5	75.0
12	Canada	72.0	70.0	74.0
13	Netherlands	72.0	69.6	74.4
14	United Kingdom	71.7	69.7	73.7
15	Norway	71.7	68.8	74.6
16	Belgium	71.6	68.7	74.6
17	Austria	71.6	68.8	74.4
18	Luxembourg	71.1	68.0	74.2
19	Iceland	70.8	69.2	72.3
20	Finland	70.5	67.2	73.7
21	Malta	70.5	68.4	72.5
22	Germany	70.4	67.4	73.5
23	Israel	70.4	69.2	71.6
24	United States	70.0	67.5	72.6

It is interesting to note that all of the five baseline countries rank well above the United States and 3 of the five rank in the top 5: Japan, France & Spain.

Healthcare Summary

Medicare for all is an interesting idea, but I'm not certain it will be as effective overall when compared to some of the other "proven" systems. It will almost immediately reduce some administrative and "profit" factors, but this will only have a small impact on costs. Baselining is the idea of not re-inventing the wheel and makes common sense. By evaluating several effective systems, it allows us to choose the very best aspects of each. In addition to evaluating the systems "process" it will be important to understand how savings can be achieved within <u>each individual component</u> that contributes to costs.

Regardless of which system is chosen (or designed), we will improve our quality of care.

Currently, we have several "special" interests that are making big money from our current system. They will not go along with any system that threatens their activity and profits. They are Insurance companies, drug companies, the legal profession, physicians, and hospitals. Achieving pricing equity even close to the five baseline countries will negatively impact significant industries. For this reason, any new system should include a "phase-in" period which would allow these industries to adjust.

Why do I say that this topic is by far the most important in the book? Following is a reprint from Chapter four and worth repeating:

"As of 2019, the per capita cost of healthcare in the US has exceeded $11,000 for every adult, child & infant. Our per capita cost is almost three times the average of the EU Countries and more than what is required for a family to provide for other essentials. Nationwide we are spending almost $3.5 trillion a year on healthcare.

If a family of four had to pay their share of this cost, they would be facing almost $44,000. Allowing for reasonable funds to provide for basic housing, food, transportation, clothing, repairs & maintenance, insurance & a modest contingency fund it is evident that anything less than a family income of $75,000 per annum will require some form of subsidy just to cover the basics.

Currently, about 1/3 of the cost is being funded by the government in the form of Medicare & Medicaid. Another 1/3 (or slightly more) is funded through company healthcare plans, and the remainder is paid by citizens in the form of premiums, deductibles, and co-pays. From a company point of view, this high cost to them reduces the funds available for wage compensation."

Our healthcare system and special interest involvement imposes a **heavy**

tax on the public in 2 ways. First, it causes Government funding for both Medicare and Medicaid to be at least $500 billion more than it should. Next, it results in insurance premiums, both for employers and private payers, to be at least 1 trillion dollars higher than they could be. Of the $3.5 trillion that is paid out annually at least $1.5 trillion of it goes into the coffers of special interests.

"Families on private health plans pay an average annual premium of $4,968 or $414 per month. The average deductible and co-pays for these plans is $ $3,879". Source: https://brandongaille.com/average-cost-private-health-insurance-per-month/

Between the premiums, the deductibles **and copays** the average family will pay almost $9, 000 per year for health insurance, and this does not include the amounts that are being provided by companies or being subsidized by the government. The regressive healthcare tax is a heavy burden on the middle class. Employers are also facing the decision to pay higher wages or continue to fund escalating insurance prices. In many cases, employers are forced to hold increases on wage levels and increase employee funding participation in insurance plans.

Assuming that we can change our system and eliminate the current $1.5 trillion in tax, the next question is how to distribute the savings. $500 billion will occur through a reduction in the current level of Medicare and Medicaid spending. The remaining $1 trillion should provide employers and private pay individuals with a reduction or elimination of premiums. That amount would add an average of $6,300 to every wage worker annually if distributed equally.

This one issue has the potential to reduce the national budget deficit to an acceptable level and at the same time, increase the average wage for the middle class.

One final comment. While the actual amount of medically related bankruptcies is in dispute, there is no doubt that it comprises a significant portion of all bankruptcy events.

CHAPTER 26:

Restoring the Middle Class and Fair Wages in Today's Economy

As detailed in earlier chapters, the middle-class is bearing an unfair financial burden resulting from the "official" tax table and the "Hidden" taxes caused by an extremely inefficient healthcare system. Also, inflation-adjusted wages have remained stagnant, while GDP per capita has nearly doubled in the past 35 years.

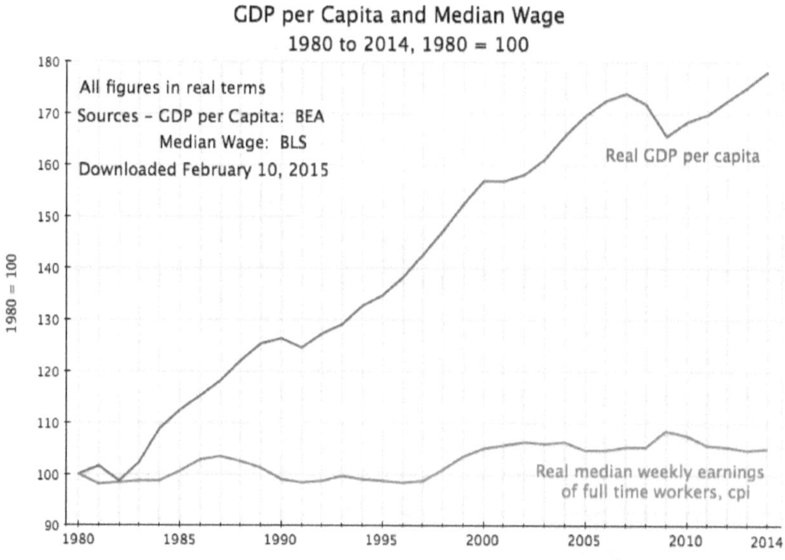

The GDP per capita trend has occurred regardless of which political party has been in control.

Source for the following: https://aneconomicsense.org/2015/02/13/why-wages-have-stagnated-while-gdp-has-grown-the-proximate-factors/

"The US has an income distribution problem. Wages have lost relative to profits (and profits largely accrue to the rich and wealthy), and the wages of lower-paid workers have fallen even while the wages of higher-paid workers have risen.

There are, therefore, two reasons for the distribution of income at the household level to have deteriorated since 1980. And one sees this in the data:"

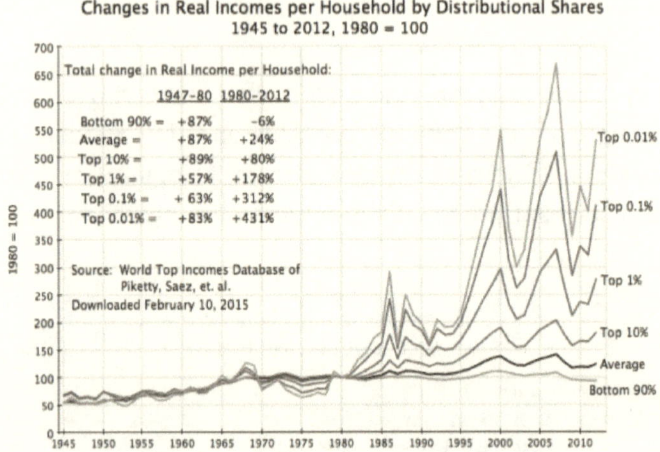

After WW II improvements in GDP were <u>fairly</u> distributed. In the early '80s, this trend changed, and since that time, almost all of the improvement in GDP has accrued to the wealthiest groups with incomes in the top 10%.

How do we solve the problem? It's relatively easy but will take the political will to change the rules. Some of the disparity would be resolved by changing our Healthcare system as detailed in a previous chapter. The other action would be to redistribute the tax burden and reduce the load borne by the middle class. More needs to be allocated to the top 10% incomes. Recommendations on a fair tax plan were contained in Chapter 23.

CHAPTER 27:

Royalty in the U.S.A and the Election Process

We need leadership. The initial idea was that those willing to serve would convey their convictions to the electorate, and the majority would decide who would guide us. While it seems that this is still what happens, the reality is a bit different. Our election process is in large part, controlled by money. I'm not saying that the candidate that has the most to spend will win, but without a large war chest, a person has little chance. The expression "*We have the best representation that money can buy*" rings true. Who has the most money to contribute to campaigns? The people at the top 1% of annual income, companies and, Super Pacs. They control a large portion of our countries wealth and have a significant influence on the outcome of elections. Any potential candidate needs to attract funds from some portion of the folks that have the wealth. To do that they will need to support certain areas of "special interest." In doing this they are allowed to become a member of our "Royalty" along with the wealthiest families and the top executives of major corporations.

I'm not naive enough to think that we can eliminate the Royals, but I am convinced that we can significantly reduce their influence. Change will require that we modify our election process and this will be extremely difficult since it will require congressional action. Our current representation will likely resist any change that would hurt their reelection chances and limit their political careers. Several other areas require change that will be next to impossible to achieve through congressional action. This and others should be candidates for a Constitutional Amendment.

How should the election process be changed? Following are some ideas that would alter the balance of power, reprinted here from chapter 22:

"One idea on term limits, which seems reasonable would be a total of 10 years of combined service (adding both House & Senate terms). Also, we should increase the house term to four years instead of the current two.

Another potential and important amendment would limit campaign terms and spending. The idea on this would be to limit all national campaigns for the executive and congressional branches to 120 days before an election and to eliminate Super PACS. Also, total spending would be capped at a level easily reached by any candidate. My thinking would be $2 million for a house seat, $5 million for a senate seat and $50 million for president. These Caps would be for the entire campaign (primaries and general elections) and would level the playing field. Also, political lobbies need to be severely restricted if not eliminated. I favor the latter, but at the very least there should be a reasonable cap on advertising and any other spending on behalf of a special interest. I'm thinking no more than $ 1 million per annum. Any campaign spending on behalf of a candidate would count against the candidate CAP."

The above actions would substantially lessen the influence of money on the outcomes of elections and allow more of the will of the electorate to become a reality.

CHAPTER 28:

Political Careers vs. Service to Country

Our founders most likely did not envision the advent of the career politician. There are several factors at work. One is the two-party system since each party wants to maintain control of each seat that they have won. History shows that the incumbent always has a better chance of victory than the challenger.

Depending on the poll Congress has somewhere between a 12 and 14% approval rating. At the same time, well over 90% of incumbents win re-election! Does this make sense?

Source for the following: https://blogs.mprnews.org/newscut/2014/11/the-power-of-the-incumbent-so-what/

"In 2014 in the House, we counted 390 incumbents who ran on Election Day. Of those, four haven't had their races called as of Nov. 10, so we'll set them aside. Of the remaining 386 incumbents, 373 won, for a winning percentage of 96.6 percent."

Another factor is that it allows the incumbent to in effect "campaign" at almost any time during the term of service:

"An incumbent usually wins an election because of the perks of his office, which

include a budget for staff in Washington, D.C. and at home, and a travel allowance, which allows him to connect with constituents while in office. Incumbents also tend to raise more money than their challengers."

And also, the incumbent is afforded substantial financial support from his or her party:

"In the November 2004 election, incumbents in the House of Representatives raised nearly $457 million, while challengers raised a little over $112 million. In the same year in the Senate race, incumbents raised just under $224 million versus just below $80 million by challengers. The average House incumbent outspent his challenger by $700,000 in 2004, and the average Senate incumbent outspent his challenger by $4 million.

In addition to money, an incumbent spends his time in office connecting with constituents, attending special events and appearing on television or radio talk shows, essentially the same activities a candidate does during a campaign. The incumbent receives a full-time wage while doing so, versus the challenger who has to find alternative ways to pay his bills while campaigning. These activities make an incumbent widely known in his district or state."

A career in National Politics ensures a successful candidate will achieve income in the top 10% for life and the wealth that accumulates with that status. Many will achieve the top 5% and higher. The initial salary or retirement is only a minor consideration. Eventually, speaking engagements, post-service job offers, and lobby participation will provide the bulk of a politician's lifetime compensation. While at least some candidates will initially enter with the best intentions, most will eventually succumb to the status and income and the lifestyle provided.

As proposed in the previous chapter term limits, campaign spending limits and benefit modifications will attract talent that wants to serve the taxpaying majority more than retaining their position.

CHAPTER 29:

The Importance of a Longer-Term Vision

Historically there have many "Super Powers." The Egyptians, Greeks, Romans, Mongolians, Harappans, and the Olmecs. Several of these thrived for over a thousand years. We have been a factor for less than 250 years and achieved the status of a world leader less than 75 years ago. During that time, the population of the Earth has tripled and is projected to exceed 10 Billion by 2050.

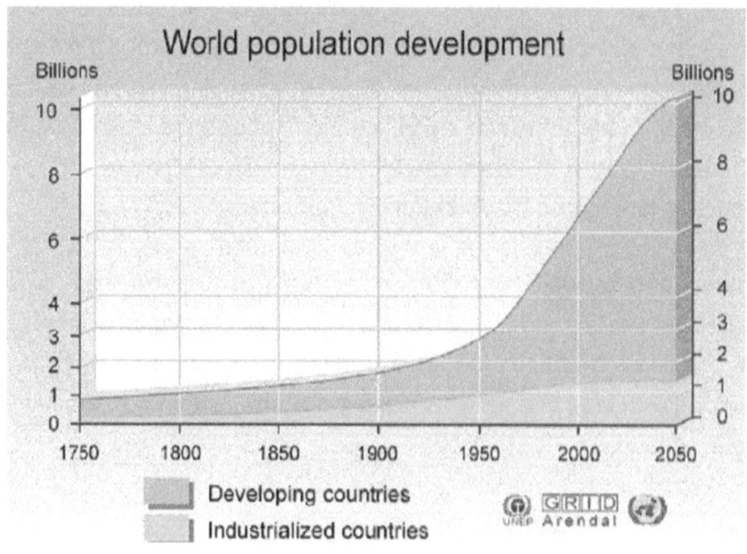

"According to the Worldwatch Institute, an environmental think tank, the Earth has <u>1.9 hectares</u> of land per person for growing food and textiles for clothing, supplying wood and absorbing waste. The average American uses about 9.7 hectares.

These data alone suggest the Earth can support at most one-fifth of the present population, 1.5 billion people, at an American standard of living."

Even at 1/3 of our standard of living, we can only sustain 4.5 billion people. Take a minute to ponder what will occur when we start running out of the necessities such as food and water. Will this provide economic stability or strife among countries? Will this be a peaceful competition? Global warming only adds to the problem for many reasons, not the least of which is the reduction of available productive farmland.

We have many issues, but globally, population growth is the most important and whatever is second pales in importance. As a world leader, we need to take a leadership position. Fortunately, we have a slightly negative internal growth rate and only slight overall growth .7% per annum as a result of immigration. Our growth rate allows us to be an example for other countries. Our current situation was not planned but has been a result of the decline in "real" wages for the middle class and the escalating costs for both healthcare and advanced education. It's just far too expensive to raise a large family. We need to do more to reduce our population. My view is that we should not incentivize families to have more than two offspring. Tax deductions should be limited to two for all but adopted children, and income security subsidies for low-income families should not exceed two children dependents.

Further, we need to take a global leadership position on this issue via the United Nations and other international and regional organizations. We need to advocate the two-child limit for all countries. Also, we need to take a leadership position regarding the actions need both internally and globally to retard the warming trend.

Source for following: https://en.wikipedia.org/wiki/
List_of_countries_by_population_growth_rate

Country Highest rate of Population Increase	2015-2020 %	Country Lowest rate of Population Increase	2015-2020 %
Bahrain	4.26	Netherlands	0.29
Oman	4.08	Taiwan	0.28
Niger	3.81	Trinidad and Tobago	0.26
Equatorial Guinea	3.59	Austria	0.24
Angola	3.28	Barbados	0.24
Uganda	3.23	Saint Vincent and the Grenadines	0.24
The Democratic Republic of the Congo	3.22	Mauritius	0.23
Burundi	3.15	Thailand	0.22
Tanzania	3.06	Germany	0.2
Chad	3.01	Syria	.02
Mali	2.99	Armenia	.015
Zambia	2.97	Albania	0.13
Gambia	2.93	Marshall Islands	0.1
Somalia	2.93	North Macedonia	0.08
Burkina Faso	2.87	Vatican City	0.8
Malawi	2.87	Slovenia	0.07
Mozambique	2.86	Cuba	0.06
	2.78		0.06
Senegal	2.77	Montenegro	0.04
Benin	2.73	Slovakia	0.04
South Sudan	2.72	Spain	0.03
Mauritania	2.69	Russia	-0.01
Madagascar	2.67	Nauru	-0.06
Congo	2.59	Italy	-0.13
Nigeria	2.58	Belarus	-0.15
Guinea	2.57	Poland	-0.17
Cameroon	2.56	Andorra	-0.21

Western Sahara (Sahrawi)	2.54	Greece	-0.21
Liberia	2.52	Bosnia and Herzegovina	-0.22
Ivory Coast	2.49	Estonia	-0.23
Kenya	2.49	Japan	-0.23
Togo	2.45	Moldova	-0.24
Guinea-Bissau	2.44	Georgia	-0.27
Ethiopia	2.43	Hungary	-0.34
Afghanistan	2.41		-0.34
Sudan	2.38	Portugal	-0.39
Qatar	2.36	Ukraine	-0.49
Rwanda	2.36	Romania	-0.50
	2.33	Lithuania	-0.55
Eritrea	2.28	Croatia	-0.58
Zimbabwe	2.28	Bulgaria	-0.67
Comoros[6]	2.24	Latvia	-1.03

All of the countries in the first column have growth rates that need curtailing. There are not enough countries in the 2nd column to offset the damage being done by column #1.

We are financially irresponsible. Both political parties have been on a spending spree as documented in Chapter 10. The current level of the National Debt is only the short-term view. We have made future financial commitments without any source of funding. The current level of UFOs (UnFunded Obligations) exceeds $125 trillion and is approaching 80% of the value of all our Assets. If today we liquidated all of our assets to fund the obligations, we would no longer be an economic power. What we have been doing is maintaining our standard of living by ignoring future obligations and passing along the consequences to future generations. As a staunch fiscal conservative this appalls me. Unless we address this issue, we will be relegated to a 2nd tier nation.

What do we need to do? The solution has already been detailed in earlier chapters and starts with changes in our election process and the healthcare system. While a balanced budget is not essential every year, it should at least balance in good economic times. In my view, our first objective would be to bring down the debt to GDP ratio down to 100% or less.

CHAPTER 30:

Out of Control
Government Spending

Where have the fiscal conservatives gone? We used to be able to count on the GOP to keep this under control. As seen in prior chapters, they have let us down. To make matters worse, approved spending in 2019 that will result in <u>more than a $1 trillion annual deficit</u> while the country is experiencing a decent increase in GDP, currently projected at 2.3 – 2.4%. We had large deficits in the past, but usually only when the economy was in recession. What is happening in 2019 is unprecedented. The economy was in ok shape before 2016, averaging a growth rate slightly over 2 %. The deficit-financed tax cut increased the growth rate to a bit over 3%, but that was merely a short-term tactic. The impact on the deficit will last for at least another ten years. The rate of growth in the economy is returning to the level of several years before 2016, and some economists are predicting a further slowdown. The growth rate for the 2nd quarter of 2019 was 2.1%.

Almost none of our elected representatives are willing to address this issue. We continue to approve budgets with no regard to the source of income. I am not opposed to a budget deficit. But when our National debt exceeds our annual GDP, I think it is past time to cut spending, especially while the economy is still robust.

How do we bring the budget in line? Several methods are suggested in prior chapters, not the least of which is to correct our healthcare system. We need to gradually change the compensation levels for federal government employees to bring them in line with the private sector. We need to have an administrative audit, by a private sector firm, for all federal government departments with productivity improvement recommendations.

CHAPTER 31:

The Bureaucracy of Government

The larger an organization, the more bureaucratic it becomes. Currently, our Government is the largest organization in our country. Funding for government operations exceeds 20 % of our GDP. While it is part of the healthcare industry, it is also larger than any industry, including healthcare.

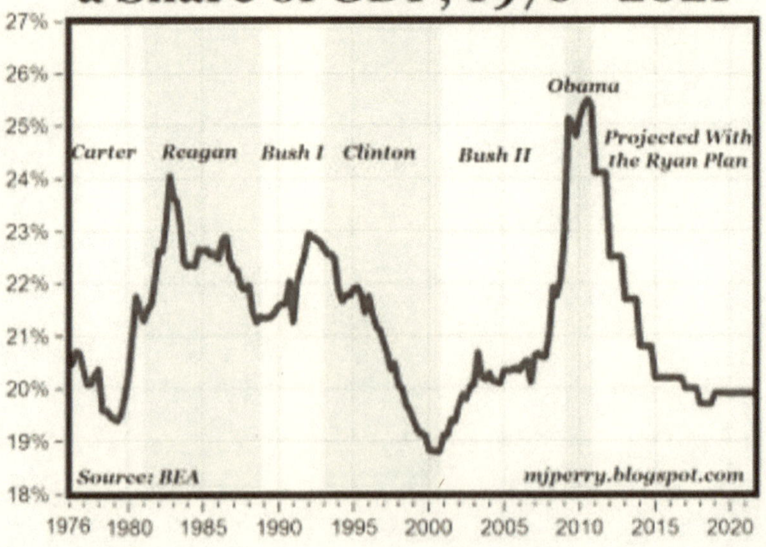

Note that it is not currently at its top rate, that was in 2010 when we were spending our way out of the recession. It hit a low at the end of the Clinton Administration and climbed throughout the Bush two terms. It peaked early in the Obama Administration, and the rest of the chart is a projection that has become a reality. The current rate stands at 21% but is again on the rise. Spending is rising at a faster rate than GDP.

Because of the size of all governments, they are inefficient. Ours is no exception. I agree that the private sector can perform many functions more efficiently, and we should encourage that idea. One area where a third party would be more efficient is in administrative auditing. Taxpayers will realize massive savings resulting from a professional, private sector audit of all employment areas, including the military.

A sure-fire recipe for inefficiency and waste is to turn an activity over to a large organization and the inevitable bureaucracy that runs the show. In our country, the largest employer by far is the Federal Government. You might speculate that there have been more government employees per capita during Democrat administrations and you would be wrong. Currently there are approximately 24 million government employees.

The following table shows the number of government employees, the total population, and the GE/P Ratio. It essentially takes a snapshot at the end of each president's term and compares it to the point when they took office. The numbers are per 1,000.

Source: http://www.forbes.com/sites/mikepatton/2013/01/24/
the-growth-of-the-federal-government-1980-to-2012/

End of Term	Date	# Government Employees (GE)	Population (P)	GE/P Ratio
Obama	Dec. 2012	21,925	315,255	6.9%
GW Bush	Dec. 2008	22,555	306,004	7.4%
Clinton	Dec. 2000	20,804	283,696	7.3%

GHW Bush	Dec. 1992	18,878	258,413	7.3%
Reagan	Dec. 1988	17,736	246,056	7.2%

The number for 2019 is 24 million GE with 329 million residents or 7.3%.

The above numbers include all those employed in all governments, federal, state & local. In total, this represents about 15% of the entire workforce (public & private). Civil service employees, which make up the bulk of Federal government employees, belong to one of (if not the) strongest unions in the country. Currently, there are just under 3 million civil service employees who represent almost 20% of all union workers. Nineteen percent of federal employees earned salaries of $100,000 or more in 2009. The average federal worker's pay was $71,208 compared with $40,331 for comparable jobs in the private sector, according to the Office of Management and Budget. In 2010, there were 82,034 workers, 3.9% of the federal workforce, making more than $150,000 annually, compared to 7,240 in 2005.

Since government workers make so much more than workers in the private-sector, one would hope that they make up the difference in productivity? Again, such thinking is misguided. The Bureau of Labor Statistics does track productivity, but one could argue that it is like the fox watching the hen house. Their stats do show a very slight annual increase in overall productivity per person (about 1% per year for the last 30 years or so). But there is a significant decrease in productivity per wages as they have increased at a faster rate. There is one very significant issue with their stats, and that is the assumption that the baseline against which all future numbers was a reasonably productive number.

Government Employees Work About One Month Less

Over the course of a calendar year, federal, state, and local government employees work about one month less than private-sector employees.

	Average Hours Worked in One Year	Hours, Compared to Private Sector	40-Hour Work Weeks, Compared to Private Sector	
Private Sector	2,083	—	—	
Federal Employees	1,930	153 fewer	3.8 fewer	
State and Local Employees	1,896	187 fewer	4.7 fewer	

Source: Author's calculations based on data from the U.S. Department of Labor, Bureau of Labor Statistics, American Time Use Survey, 2003–2010, http://www.bls.gov/tus/ (accessed August 31, 2012).

B 2724 ☎ heritage.org

The above chart is revealing, but it still does not address the issue of productivity of the individual in the workplace. What it does reflect is that government workers make 75%+ more than private-sector workers and work 10% fewer hours. Potential improvement from an audit is a very difficult item on which to find valid information, so I speculate a bit. I would be willing to bet all of the money in my bank account that a 10%+ improvement in individual productivity among all government workers is achievable. I suspect this expectation is too low. Achieving this result will never occur through any inspection or evaluation by an existing government agency. We need the help of unbiased auditors. As pointed out in earlier chapters, we need to bring the federal wage scale in line with the private sector. The change should occur slowly over time to allow existing employees to adjust.

CHAPTER 32

Capitalism & Free Markets

I favor both the capitalistic system and free global markets. Capitalism works best in free markets. If one country is more productive than others in a particular industry or product line, then they deserve to gain a larger market share. In the long term, productivity and quality will determine market position.

Cheap labor tends to place some countries at a short-term advantage. In many instances, a lack of capital tends to level the playing field. Projecting longer term, emerging economies will find wages rising as well as the availability of capital. I repeat, <u>eventually productivity and quality will determine market position</u>. Countries with smaller populations will be forced to focus their efforts on a limited number of industries to remain competitive.

Protectionism is not in any countries' best interest. Any country that chooses to protect its domestic market will find that other countries will have no choice but to retaliate. Protectionist countries will lose out in the long run and hamper the standard of living for their citizens.

CHAPTER 33:

Monetary vs Fiscal Policy

Below is from Wikipedia

"In economics and political science, fiscal policy is the use of government revenue collection and expenditure to influence a country's economy. The use of government revenues and expenditures to influence macroeconomic variables developed as a result of the Great Depression when the previous laissez-faire approach to economic management became discredited. Fiscal policy is based on the theories of the British economist John Maynard Keynes. Keynesian economics indicated that government changes in the levels of taxation and government spending influences aggregate demand and the level of economic activity. Fiscal and monetary policy are the key strategies used by a country's government and central bank to advance its economic objectives. The combination of these policies enables these authorities to target inflation and to increase employment. Additionally, it is designed to try to keep GDP growth at 2%–3% and the unemployment rate near the natural unemployment rate of 4%–5%. This implies that fiscal policy is used to stabilize the economy throughout the business cycle.

Monetary policy is the process by which the monetary authority of a country controls the supply of money. Often targeting an inflation rate or interest rate to ensure price stability and general trust in the currency."

Both techniques can only prop up the economy in the short term, but the short term in the case of monetary policy can mean a decade or more. A case in point is the historically low-interest rates of the last decade.

Below from "The balance"

Fed Chair Ben Bernanke (February 2006—January 2014)

Date	GDP rate %	Fed Funds rate %	Unemployment rate %	Inflation %	Significant events/ comments
Jan-06	2.90%	4.50%	6%	2.50%	Raised to cool housing market bubble. More homeowners default.
Mar-06		4.75%			"
May-06		5.00%			"
Mar-07	1.90%	5.25%	6%	4.10%	Home sales fell
Sep-07		4.75%			
Oct-07		4.50%			
Dec-07		4.25%			**LIBOR** rose. **Stock market peaked. Recession began.**
Jan-08	0.10%	3.50%	6%	0.10%	
Jan-08		3.00%			Tax rebate.
Mar-08		2.25%			Bear Stearns bailout.
Apr-08		2.00%			Lehman fails. Bank bailout approved. AIG bailout.
Oct-08		1.50%			^
Oct-08		1.00%			^
Dec-08		0.25%			Effectively zero. Lowest fed fund rates possible
Dec-08		0%			

Between 08 & 15 the Fed kept the rate at 0%					Recession ended in June 2009
Dec-15	2.90%	0.50%	6%	0.70%	Growth stabilized so Fed began raising rates.
Dec-16	1.60%	0.75%	4.60%	2.10%	Fed maintained steady rate
Mar-17	2.40%	1.00%	4.10%	2.10%	Fed was steady on its path of normalizing its benchmark rate.
Jun-17		1.25%			
Dec-17		1.50%			
Fed Chair Jerome Powell (Since February 2018)					
Mar-18	2.90%	1.75%	3.90%	1.90%	Fed projects steady growth.
Jun-18		2.00%			"
Sep-18		2.25%			"
Dec-18		2.50%			Fed promised to stop raising rates.
Jul-19	2.10%	2.25%	3.70%	2.00%	Fed lowered rate despite steady growth.

The track record indicates that the lowering of interest rates was systematic during the onset of the recession and then very slowly raised as the economy improved. With the economy showing stabilized growth and employment and inflation at more than acceptable rates, why was the Fed rate lowered in July 2019? In good times during the decade preceding the 2008 recession, the average Fed funds rate exceeded 4%. Other countries have funds rates lower than the U.S., but their economies are not as robust as ours. In previous chapters, the status of our fiscal policy has been sufficiently documented. Despite a robust economy, we are running record deficits that will exceed $1 trillion for 2019.

Both monetary and fiscal policies are being used improperly to bolster the economy. Neither policy can be maintained indefinitely, and it will eventually lead to a slow down and possibly a recession. What should happen in a good economy is stable or slight increases in funds rates and, low deficits or in some cases budget surpluses. The mis-management of both fiscal and monetary policies over the past several years has been very short-term thinking. The economy will pay a severe price soon.

CHAPTER 34:

Actions required to reinstate our status as a respected World Leader

- Ratify an Equal Rights Amendment
- Establish Congressional term limits
- Severely limit or abolish lobbyists
- Revise, severely limit, and enforce campaign donations
- Reduce election campaigning time to no more than four months.
- Revise and simplify the income tax code to eliminate most tax loop-holes (deductions) and reduce the burden on the middle class. Revise brackets to move the tax burden from the middle class and onto the top 10% of incomes. Limit dependent deductions to two.
- Restrict our military involvement to defense and terrorist prevention. Resign our role as the "world cop".
- Re-design our healthcare system using successful European systems as model resources.
- Increase minimum wage to one that provides for necessities at a minimum. Allow for exceptions for persons under the age of 18 and provide a phase-in to minimum for first-time employees.
- Limit low-income subsidies to two dependents
- Initiate a 3rd party audit of all government administrative departments and implement their cost savings recommendations. The audit would include a comparative wage evaluation.

- Provide Congressional guidelines for fiscal policy that would include deficit limits during stable economic periods.
- Provide enhanced congressional oversight to ensure the FED is not influenced by political agendas.

www.ingramcontent.com/pod-product-compliance
Lightning Source LLC
Chambersburg PA
CBHW051104250726
48656CB00001B/459